HOW TO PRAY EFFECTIVELY

UPDATED FOR TODAY'S READERS WITH
INTRODUCTION AND STUDY GUIDE

R. A. TORREY

GODLIPRESS TEAM

© **Copyright 2021 by GodliPress.**

All rights reserved. The content contained within this book may not be reproduced, duplicated, or transmitted without direct written permission from the author or the publisher, except in the case of brief quotations embodied in critical articles or reviews.

Scripture quotations are from The ESV® Bible (The Holy Bible, English Standard Version®), copyright © 2001 by Crossway, a publishing ministry of Good News Publishers. Used by permission. All rights reserved.

CONTENTS

Introduction	vii
1. THE IMPORTANCE OF PRAYER	1
There Is A Devil	2
The Way For Us To Receive Things	3
The Most Important Duty In The Disciples' Lives	4
A Vital Part Of Jesus' Life On Earth	4
The Most Important Part Of Jesus' Present Ministry	5
To Receive Mercy And Grace	7
To Find Joy	8
To Find Peace And Freedom From Worry	9
To Receive The Holy Spirit	11
To Keep Us Clear-Minded Until Jesus Returns	13
For What It Fulfills	14
Study Questions	18
2. PRAYING TO GOD	20
To God	20
Without Stopping	22
By The Church	24
Study Questions	25
3. OBEYING AND PRAYING	27
Whatever He Asks	27
What Pleases Him	29
In Truth	30
Study Questions	32

4. PRAYING IN JESUS' NAME ACCORDING TO
   GOD'S WILL   34
   In His Name   34
   In Confidence   37
   Study Questions   41

5. PRAYING IN THE SPIRIT   43
   In The Spirit   43
   With Faith   45
   Study Questions   46

6. ALWAYS PRAYING AND NOT GIVING UP   48
   Study Questions   51

7. ABIDING IN JESUS   52
   Abide In Me   52
   My Words Abide In You   54
   Study Questions   55

8. PRAY WITH THANKSGIVING   57
   Study Questions   59

9. OBSTACLES TO PRAYER   61
   Your Own Desires   61
   Our Sins   63
   Idols Of The Heart   65
   Ignoring The Poor   66
   Unforgiveness   67
   Division In The Marriage   68
   Doubt   69
   Study Questions   69

10. WHEN TO PRAY   71
    In The Morning   71
    All Night   72
    Before Important Events   73
    After Success   74
    In Very Busy Times   75
    In Temptation   76
    At All Times   77
    Study Questions   78

11. THE NEED FOR GLOBAL REVIVAL	79
The Results In A Minister	81
The Results In Christians	82
The Results In The Lost	83
Why A Revival Is Necessary	84
Study Questions	89
12. PRAY BEFORE AND DURING REVIVALS	91
Study Questions	99
About R. A. Torrey	101
References	105

INTRODUCTION

Prayer is not something strange or foreign. These days it is embraced, even encouraged by everyone from Buddhists, New Agers, psychologists, politicians, and even celebrities. Instead of praying as Jesus did, it has come to mean a calm oneness with a distant, higher being or merely a sign of sympathy for others. We hear phrases like, "Our prayers are with you," or "We'll be praying for you," everywhere we go.

These words have become so common, we even hear politicians use such phrases on television after or during a tragedy. Words like these seem to fall off people's lips so easily today. We even say it out of respect, but seldom even go through with the act of actual praying. Prayer has become an accepted part of society, where people think or hope that a higher being will somehow correct the wrongs of the universe. But this is not prayer!

As Christians, prayer is the lifeblood of our relationship with Jesus. It is our connection to the Father. The belief that He can hear our hearts, and we can know His will for our lives. There is nothing more intimate and powerful. The problem is that many of us have drifted from what prayer should be, to what the world has accepted and made it out to be. Our prayer lives have lost their power and their intimacy to become nothing more than expectant shopping lists and get-out-of-jail cards.

Thankfully, we have a book like this to guide us back onto the right biblical track.

How to Pray Effectively was written by Torrey in 1900, more than 100 years ago. Besides being an active pastor and evangelist, he was also an avid author and went on to write over forty books covering an array of topics, such as revivals and how to conduct them, the Holy Spirit in our lives, reading the Bible for our spiritual growth, and other important topics that Christians need to know and understand. This one has stood out over the years as a favorite for many Christian workers, a go-to for answers, and a definitive guide on the subject of prayer.

Torrey seemed to understand that most people, especially more so today, don't have time to spend trying to figure out the meanings or haven't got the energy for deep theological dissertations— they just want the answers. It is probably the reason most of his books have titles beginning with "How to…" They served more as handbooks and manuals for the busy Christian.

This one is no exception. It is filled with clear, easy-to-find headings, answers, and verses. Torrey knew how and wanted certain words and phrases to stand out and catch our attention. More than that, though, is being able to learn from those who have walked the path and fought the fight. The stories and examples are vivid and challenging for our own lives.

R.A. Torrey was undoubtedly one of the mighty men of God of the early 20th century that helped shape, guide, and shine a light for churches and Christians to follow. His passion and determination were as potent back then as they are today—as you'll read in this book. This passion is why the pages are filled with rich, deep wisdom that makes this a timeless manual on how to pray.

Such a precious book needs to be made available to this generation. We need to be able to read and understand the importance of prayer for our lives today in our world now. So with care and consideration, this classic has been updated into English that is easier for us to read, while ensuring Torrey's message remains the same now as it was in 1900. Study questions have been added, not because the book is unclear or weak on its own, but simply as a guide into deeper thought on what has already been written.

If you are looking for answers—as we all are— and if you are seeking a deeper relationship with God, then *How to Pray Effectively* will challenge you to reach your desires. This book will help you to see prayer as a priority in your walk with the Lord. It will also help you to see that there is much more in store for those that seek Jesus with all their hearts in prayer.

As Torrey often said, "Pray it through."

1

THE IMPORTANCE OF PRAYER

In Ephesians 6:18 we read words that show the incredible importance of prayer very clearly and forcefully:

"Praying at all times in the Spirit, with all prayer and supplication. To that end, keep alert with all perseverance, making supplication for all the saints."

When we really stop to understand the meaning of these words and their context, we will say, "I must pray, pray, pray. I must put all my energy and all my heart into prayer. Whatever else I do, I must pray."

Note the use of the word all: *"at all times," "with all prayer," "with all perseverance," "for all the saints."* Note all the strong words: *"prayer," "supplication," "perseverance."* See the strong expression: *"keep alert."*

Paul realized that humans are naturally lazy, especially towards prayer. How seldom we pray things through! How often do the church and the individual get right to the verge of a great blessing in prayer and just then let go, get drowsy, and quit? I wish that these words *"keep alert"* would burn into our hearts. I wish the whole verse would burn into our hearts.

But why is this constant, persistent, sleepless, overcoming prayer so needful?

There Is A Devil

He is cunning, mighty, and never rests. He is always plotting the downfall of those belonging to God. If the child of God relaxes in prayer, the devil will succeed in catching him.

This is the thought of the context as we read in Eph 6:12-13:

"For we do not wrestle against flesh and blood, but against the rulers, against the authorities, against the cosmic powers over this present darkness, against the spiritual forces of evil in the heavenly places. Therefore take up the whole armor of God, that you may be able to withstand in the evil day, and having done all, to stand firm."

Next follows a description of the different parts of the Christian's armor, which we must put on to stand against the devil and his cunning tricks. Then Paul brings it to a climax in verse 18; telling us that on top of everything else, we must add prayer— constant, persistent, untiring, sleepless prayer in the Holy Spirit, or everything else counts for nothing.

The Way For Us To Receive Things

A second reason for this constant, persistent, sleepless, overcoming prayer is that prayer is God's way for us to receive things. The secret of why we lack in our experience, our life, and our work is that we neglect prayer.

In James 4:2, this point is made very clear: *"You do not have, because you do not ask."* These words contain the secret of the poverty and powerlessness of the average Christian—neglecting prayer.

Many Christians ask, "Why do I make so little progress in my spiritual life?"

"Neglecting prayer," God answers. "You do not have because you do not ask."

Many ministers ask, "Why do I see so little fruit from all my work?"

Again God answers, "Neglecting prayer. You do not have because you do not ask."

Many Sunday-School teachers ask, "Why do I see so few becoming born again in my Sunday-school class?"

Still, God answers, "Neglecting prayer. You do not have because you do not ask."

Preachers and churches ask, "Why does the church of Christ make so little progress against unbelief, error, sin, and worldliness?"

Once more we hear God answering, "Neglecting prayer. You do not have because you do not ask."

The Most Important Duty In The Disciples' Lives

Thirdly, let us remember that the apostles were God's example of what He expected Christians to be— with prayer as the most important duty of their lives.

When the growing responsibilities of the early church got too much for them, they *"summoned the full number of the disciples and said, 'It is not right that we should give up preaching the word of God to serve tables. Therefore, brothers, pick out from among you seven men of good repute, full of the Spirit and of wisdom, whom we will appoint to this duty. But <u>we will devote ourselves to prayer and to the ministry of the word.</u>'"* (Acts 6:2-4)

It is evident from what Paul wrote to the churches and individuals about praying for them, that a lot of his time, strength, and thought was given to prayer. (see Rom 1:9, Eph 1:15-16; Col 1:9, 1 Thess 3:10, 2 Tim 1:3)

All the mighty men of God outside the Bible have been men of prayer. They have differed from one another in many things, but in this one thing, they have been the same.

A Vital Part Of Jesus' Life On Earth

Furthermore this constant, persistent, sleepless, overcoming prayer played an incredibly important role in Jesus' life on Earth.

In Mark 1:35 we read, *"And rising very early in the morning, while it was still dark, he departed and went out to a desolate place, and there he prayed."* The day before that had been a very busy and exciting one, but Jesus cut back on the hours needed for sleep so that He might wake early and spend more time in prayer.

Turn to Luke 6:12, where we read, *"In these days he went out to the mountain to pray, and all night he continued in prayer to God."* Jesus sometimes found it necessary to take a whole night for prayer.

The words "pray" and "prayer" are used at least twenty-five times in connection with Jesus in the four Gospels. You will find prayer took much of the time and strength of Jesus. A man or woman who does not spend much time in prayer cannot properly be called a follower of Jesus Christ.

The Most Important Part Of Jesus' Present Ministry

Jesus' ministry did not end with His death. His atoning work was finished on the cross, but when He rose and ascended to the right hand of the Father, He entered into other work just as important. The two cannot be separated. The one is the foundation for the other, but both are necessary for our complete salvation.

Therefore, praying is the most important part of our Risen Lord's ministry today.

We can read about this present work that brings our salvation to completeness in Heb. 7:25, *"Consequently, he is able to save to the uttermost those who draw near to God through him, since he always lives to make intercession for them."* This verse tells us that Jesus is able to save us to the uttermost, not just *from* the uttermost, but *to* the uttermost. We are brought to entire completeness, absolute perfection because He not only died but because He also *"always lives."* It also tells us what purpose He now lives for, *"to make intercession for us."* To pray. Praying is the main thing He is doing. It is by His prayers that He is saving us.

The same thought is found in Paul's amazing, triumphant challenge in Rom. 8:34. *"Who is to condemn? Christ Jesus is the one who died—more than that, who was raised—who is at the right hand of God, who indeed is interceding for us."*

If we are to have fellowship with Jesus in His present work, we must spend a lot of time in prayer. We must spend time in sincere, constant, persistent, sleepless, overcoming prayer. There is nothing that shows me how important praying at all times is, as much as realizing that it is the main occupation right now of my risen Lord. I want to have fellowship with Him. And so I have asked that whatever the Father wants to make me, that He will make me an intercessor— a man who knows how to pray and who spends much time in prayer.

This ministry of intercession is a glorious and mighty service, and we can all take part in it. The man or woman who cannot be at a public meeting because of sickness can still be a part of it. The busy mother looking after her children, or the woman who has to take in washing can take part in praying for other Christians, her pastor, the unsaved, and for foreign missionaries as she watches her kids or completes her chores. The hard-driven businessman can be part of it, praying as he rushes from meeting to meeting. But of course, we must, to keep this spirit of constant prayer, take time. Take plenty of this precious time when we withdraw alone to a secret place with God for no other reason than prayer.

To Receive Mercy And Grace

Constant, persistent, sleepless, overcoming prayer is the way God made for us to receive mercy and grace in our time of need.

Heb. 4:16 is one of the simplest and sweetest verses in the Bible—*"Let us then with confidence draw near to the throne of grace, that we may receive mercy and find grace to help in time of need."* These words make it very clear that God has made a way for us to find and receive mercy and grace. That way is prayer. Prayer is our bold, confident approach to the throne of grace, the most holy place of God's presence, where our High Priest, Jesus Christ, has entered for us. (Heb 4:14-15.)

Mercy is what we need, grace is what we must have, or all our life and effort will end in complete failure. Prayer is the way to get them. The measure of grace we receive is determined by the measure of our prayers. There is an endless supply of grace for us, and we make it ours by prayer. If we only realized the fullness of God's grace available to us if we ask for it— how high, deep, long, and wide His grace is.— If we realize this, I am sure we would spend more time in prayer.

Who doesn't feel that they need more grace? Then ask for it. Be constant and persistent in your asking. God loves us to be "shameless" beggars when it comes to grace. For it shows our faith in Him, and faith pleases Him. Because of our "shamelessness," He will give us as much as we need (Luke 11:8). What little streams of mercy and grace most of us know, when we could know rivers that overflow their banks!

To Find Joy

This type of prayer is also the way Jesus created for those who follow Him to receive the fullness of joy.

He says it simply and beautifully in John 16:24, *"Until now you have asked nothing in my name. Ask, and you will receive, that your joy may be full."* Who does not wish their joy to be made full? The way to have it filled to the top is by praying in the name of Jesus. We all know people whose joy is full, running over, shining from their eyes, bubbling out of their lips, and running off their fingertips when they shake hands with you. Coming into contact with them is like coming into contact with an electrical machine charged with gladness. People with this energy are always people that spend lots of time in prayer.

Why is it that prayer in the name of Christ brings such fullness of joy? Partly, because we get what we ask. But that is not the only reason, nor the greatest. It makes God real. When we ask something definite of God, and He gives it, how real God becomes! He is right there! It is incredible to have a God who is real, and not just an idea of Him.

I remember how I once became suddenly and seriously sick in my study. I dropped to my knees and cried to God for help.

Instantly all pain left me— I was perfectly well. It seemed as if God stood right there, and had put out His hand and touched me. The joy of the healing was not as great as the joy of meeting God.

There is no greater joy on earth or in heaven, than fellowship with God; prayer in the name of Jesus brings us into fellowship with Him. The person who wrote the Psalms was not speaking only of future joy, but also present joy when they said,

"In your presence there is fullness of joy." (Ps. 16.11.) Oh, the indescribable joy of those moments when we truly press into the presence of God in our prayers!

If you desire to experience this joy ask yourself these questions: "I have never known such joy as I have during prayer"? Do you take enough time for prayer to actually get into God's presence? Do you really give yourself up to prayer in those times? Only then can this real joy begin.

To Find Peace And Freedom From Worry

Next, let's remember that constant and deep prayer is the way God has given us to find His peace that passes all understanding and freedom from all anxiety.

"Do not be anxious about anything," says Paul, *"but in everything by prayer and supplication with thanksgiving let your requests be made known to God. And the peace of God, which surpasses all understanding, will guard your hearts and your minds in Christ Jesus."* (Phil. 4:6-7.) At first glance, many see this as the picture of a beautiful life that is beyond reach for normal people like us.

This is not true. The verse also tells us how every child of God can achieve it: *"Do not be anxious about anything."* The rest of the verse tells us how, and it is very simple: *"But in everything by prayer and supplication with thanksgiving let your requests be made known to God."* What could be plainer or more simple than that?

Just keep in constant touch with God, and when any trouble or irritation comes up, big or small, speak to Him about it, never forgetting to give thanks for what He has already done. What will the result be? *"And the peace of God, which surpasses all understanding, will guard your hearts and your minds in Christ Jesus."*

That is wonderful. And it is just as simple. Thank God, many are trying it. Don't you know anyone who is always calm? Perhaps he is naturally a very stormy man, but troubles, conflicts, setbacks, and loss may sweep around him, and the peace of God that passes all understanding guards his heart and thoughts in Christ Jesus.

We all know such people. How do they manage it?

Just by prayer, that's all. Those people who know the deep peace of God, the bottomless peace that passes all understanding, are always men and women of much prayer.

Some of us let the fast pace of our lives crowd prayer out—what a waste of time and energy there is from the constant worry! One night of prayer will save us from many nights of insomnia. Time spent in prayer is not wasted, but time invested with huge interest.

To Receive The Holy Spirit

Prayer is a method God has given us that grants our ability to obtain the Holy Spirit.

The Bible is very clear on this point. Jesus says, *"If you then, who are evil, know how to give good gifts to your children, how much more will the heavenly Father give the Holy Spirit to those who ask him!"* (Luke 11:13.) These days we are told by very good people, "You must not pray for the Holy Spirit." But what then do they make of the plain statement of Jesus Christ—*"How much more will the heavenly Father give the Holy Spirit to those that ask him!"*

Some years ago just before giving a sermon on the baptism of the Holy Spirit, someone came to me very worked up and said,

"Make sure you don't tell them to pray for the Holy Spirit."

"I will most definitely tell them to do it, for Jesus says, 'How much more shall the heavenly Father give the Holy Spirit to those that ask Him."

"Oh, yes," he replied, "but that was before Pentecost."

"How about Acts 4:31? Was that before Pentecost or after?"

"After, of course."

"Read it."

"'*And when they had prayed, the place in which they were gathered together was shaken, and they were all filled with the Holy Spirit and continued to speak the word of God with boldness.*'"

"How about Acts 8:15? Was that before Pentecost or after?"

"After."

"Please read."

"*'Who came down and prayed for them that they might <u>receive the Holy Spirit</u>.'*"

He didn't answer. What could he answer? It is very clear in the Word of God that before Pentecost and after, the baptism and infilling of the Holy Spirit were received in answer to definite prayer.

Experience also teaches this. Many have probably received the Holy Spirit the same moment they surrendered to God before there was time to pray. But many know that their first baptism of the Holy Spirit came while they were on their knees or faces before God, alone or with others. And since then, they have been filled with the Holy Spirit in the place of prayer again and again!

I know this just as much as my thirst has been quenched while I was drinking water. Early one morning in the Chicago Avenue Church prayer room, where several hundred people had gathered to pray for several hours, the Holy Spirit filled the whole place with His presence so heavily that no one could speak or pray— only sobs of joy filled the place. Men left that room to go to different parts of the country by train, and reports soon came back of the outpouring of God's Holy Spirit in answer to prayer. Others went into the city with the blessing of God upon them. In my own experience, this is only one of the many times such an event has happened.

If we would only spend more time in prayer, there would be more of the Spirit's power in our work. Many who once worked in the power of the Holy Spirit are now filling the air with empty shouts and meaningless gestures because they have let prayer be crowded out by other things. We must spend much time on our knees before God if we are to continue in the power of the Holy Spirit.

To Keep Us Clear-Minded Until Jesus Returns

Furthermore, prayer is the way Christ has given to us to keep our hearts from indulging so much in life's cares that we will be unprepared when He returns.

One of the most interesting and honest passages on prayer in the Bible is Luke 21:34-36: *"But watch yourselves lest your hearts be weighed down with dissipation and drunkenness and cares of this life, and that day come upon you suddenly like a trap. For it will come upon all who dwell on the face of the whole earth. But stay awake at all times, praying that you may have strength to escape all these things that are going to take place, and to stand before the Son of Man."* According to this passage, there is only one way in which we can be prepared for the coming of the Lord when He appears — through much prayer.

The return of Jesus Christ is a subject that is catching the interest of many people and causing much discussion. But it is one thing to be interested in the Lord's return and to talk about it, but quite another thing to be prepared for it. We live in a society that constantly makes us ill-equipped for His coming. The world draws us down by its pleasures and interests.

There is only one way we can rise above these things— by constant prayer, by becoming alert, and awake in prayer. The words used by Luke, "watch," and "all times," are the same strong words used in Eph. 6:18. The man who spends little time in prayer, who is not steadfast and constant in it, will not be ready for the Lord when He comes. But we can be ready. How? Pray! Pray! Pray!

For What It Fulfills

The final reason for constant, persistent, sleepless, overcoming prayer is a mighty one: because of what prayer accomplishes. Much has been said on this already, but there is more that can be added.

Prayer Encourages Growth

Prayer promotes our spiritual growth like nothing else can. (Except maybe studying the Bible.) True prayer and true Bible study go hand in hand.

It is through prayer that my sin is revealed, my most hidden sin. As I kneel before God and pray, *"Search me, O God, and know my heart! Try me and know my thoughts! And see if there be any grievous way in me,"* (Ps.139:23-24). God shoots the penetrating rays of His light into the deepest corners of my heart, and the sins I never suspected are revealed.

In answer to prayer, God washes me from my wickedness and cleanses me from my sin (Ps. 51:2). In answer to prayer, my eyes are opened to see wonderful things in God's Word (Ps. 119:18). In answer to prayer, I get the wisdom to know God's way (Jas. 1:5). I receive the strength to walk in it. As I meet

God in prayer and gaze into His face, I am changed into His own image from glory to glory (2 Cor. 3:18). Each day of true prayer finds me becoming more like Jesus.

John Welch, John Knox's son-in-law, was one of the most faithful men of prayer this world ever saw. A day was wasted if seven or eight hours were not spent alone with God in prayer and the study of His Word. An old man speaking of him after his death said, "He was a type of Christ."

How did he become like that? His prayer life explains the mystery.

Prayer Brings Power Into Our Work

If we want power for the work God calls us to do we can get it by sincere prayer. Whether that work is preaching, teaching, personal work, or raising our children, we must pray.

A woman with a nasty, badly-behaved little boy, once came to me in desperation and said, "What shall I do with him?"

I asked, "Have you ever tried prayer?"

She said that she had prayed for him. I asked if she had prayed specifically and expectantly about his salvation and character. She replied that she had not. She began that day, and at once there was a significant change in the child, and he grew up as a mature Christian.

How many Sunday-school teachers have taught for months and years, seen no real fruit from their efforts; then learned the secret of intercession, and by sincere pleading with God, have seen the children brought to Christ! How many poor preachers have become mighty men of God by laying down their own ability and gifts, to surrender and wait on God for the power only he can give! John Livingstone spent a night with others in prayer and conversation. When he preached the next day in the Kirk of Shotts, five hundred people were converted or showed significant growth in their lives. Prayer and power are inseparable.

Prayer Helps In People Getting Saved

Few converts have come to know Jesus that have not done so without someone having prayed for them. I used to think that nobody else had anything to do with my conversion because I was not born again in church, Sunday school, or in connection with anyone else. I woke up in the middle of the night and was converted. As far as I can remember, I didn't even have any thoughts of being converted or anything else to do with it.

I was woken up in the middle of the night in my bed and was born again in about five minutes. Just before that, I was as near to hell as someone can get, with one foot over the edge. I thought no one else had anything to do with my salvation, but I had forgotten about my mother's prayers. Later, I found out that one of my college classmates had chosen to pray for me until I was saved.

Prayer often works when everything else fails. St. Augustine's mother's efforts to try and deal with her boy had failed, but her prayers won through— the rebellious child became a mighty man of God. By prayer the worst enemies of the Gospel have become its strongest defenders, the greatest criminals have become the truest sons of God, and the most offensive women have become the purest saints. Oh, the power of prayer to reach down, down, down, where hope itself seems lost, and lift men and women up, up, up into fellowship with and likeness to God. It is simply wonderful! How little we appreciate this marvelous weapon!

Prayer Brings Blessings To The Church

The history of the church has always been one of the incredible difficulties to overcome. The devil hates the church and tries to block its progress every chance he can; by false doctrine, division, and corrupting people. But by prayer, a clear way can be made through everything. Prayer will root out heresy, decrease misunderstanding, sweep away jealousy and hate, wipe out wickedness, and bring in the full flow of God's reviving grace. History proves this again and again. In the darkest hours, when the church has seemed beyond hope, believing men and women have met together, cried to God, and the answer has come.

It was the same in the days of Knox, Wesley, Whitfield, Edwards, Brainerd, and Finney. It was the same in the 1857 revival in America and the 1859 revival in Ireland. It will be the same in your day and mine.

Satan has gathered his forces. Christian science lifts its head high with its false Christ— a woman. Others loudly claim new apostolic teachings, only to cover up their dishonesty and hypocrisy. Christians following the truths of the Gospel are glaring at each other with a devilish suspicion. The world, the flesh, and the devil are rampant. It is now a dark day.

But now *"it is time for the Lord to act, for your law has been broken."* (Ps. 119:126). And He is getting ready to work, and He is listening for the voice of prayer. Will He hear it? Will He hear it from you? Will He hear it from the church as a body? I believe He will.

Study Questions

There is so much to digest in this chapter. Take time, even to write down the 11 key points of constant, persistent, sleepless, overcoming prayer again so that you can see them easily and clearly before you. Use the questions below to help you sort through, think more in-depth, and challenge your ideas on why prayer is so important. Make sure your Bible is close so that you can refer to verses to help you.

Don't rush through the questions, and don't feel that you need to stick to them in order, or even answer every single one. They are only to serve as a guide to help you explore the ideas that have been spoken about already.

1. If you had to choose just one aspect of why prayer is so important from Torrey's list, which one stands out to you most? Why?
2. Which one do you struggle to understand or accept the most?
3. What does James 4:2 mean to you?
4. What is your opinion of point number 9, receiving the Holy Spirit?
5. Is the Holy Spirit relevant in our lives today? Is the Holy Spirit relevant for the church today?

6. Looking at number 11 on what prayer accomplishes, which one of the points he makes would you say is the most important aspect that prayer fulfills?
7. How important is prayer in your own life? If you had to rate it out of 10 (1-not much, 10-can't live without it), where would it rank?

2
PRAYING TO GOD

We have seen the importance and power of prayer, so now we come directly to the question— how to pray with power.

To God

In Acts chapter 12, we find a prayer that prevailed with God and brought great results. In verse 5, the manner and method of this prayer are described:

"But earnest prayer for him was made to God by the church," (Acts 12:5).

The first thing to notice here is the phrase, "to God." The prayer that has power is the prayer that is offered to God.

But some will say, "Is not all prayer to God?"

No. A lot of so-called prayers are not to God. For a prayer to be to God, there must be a definite and conscious approach to God; we must have a clear awareness that God is bending over and listening as we pray. In most of our prayers, there is little thought of God. Our mind is filled with what we need, and not with the mighty, loving Father whom we are asking. Often we are not even thinking of either of those— and word our mind is simply wandering everywhere else. There is no power in that sort of prayer. But when we really come into God's presence, really meet Him face to face in the place of prayer, really seek the things that we desire *from Him*, then there is power.

If we want to pray correctly, the first thing we should do is to meet with God. Get into His very presence. Before we ask for anything, we should have a clear understanding that we are talking to God, and believe that He is listening and going to give us what we ask for. This is only possible by the Holy Spirit's power. So, we should not be quick with our words, but wait until the Holy Spirit leads us into the presence of God.

One night an active Christian dropped into a prayer meeting that I was leading. Before we knelt to pray, I said something like the above, telling everyone to be sure before they prayed and while they were praying that they were really in God's presence. I reminded them that they should be more mindful of the Lord than of their prayers. A few days later I met this man again, and he said that he had never heard this simple thought before and it had made prayer a completely new experience for him.

If we should pray correctly, these two little words must sink deep into our hearts: "To God."

Without Stopping

The second secret of effective praying is found in the same verse, in the words "earnest."

In other versions, it is written as "constant" or "without ceasing." None of these capture the original strength of the word in Greek. It means "stretched-out-ed-ly." It is a very graphic and expressive word. It represents the soul on a stretch of earnest and intense desire. "Intensely" would translate it better. It is the same word used in Luke 22:44 where it says, Jesus *"prayed more earnestly; and his sweat became like great drops of blood falling down to the ground."*

In Heb. 5:7 we read that *"In the days of his flesh, Jesus offered up prayers and supplications, with loud cries and tears,"* In Rom. 15:30, Paul begs the Christians in Rome to strive together with him in their prayers. The translation of the word, "strive" means to take part in athletic games or a fight. In other words, the effective prayer is the one into which we put our whole soul, stretching out toward God in intense and agonizing desire.

Many of our prayers these days have no power in them, because there is no heart in them. We rush into God's presence, run through a string of requests, jump up, and go out. If someone should ask us what we had just prayed for, we probably would not be able to remember. If we put so little heart into our prayers, we cannot expect God to put much heart into answering them.

There is a lot of mention about the rest of faith, but there is also the fight of faith in prayer and effort. Those who would like us to think that they have reached great faith and trust without any agony of conflict and prayer, have run straight past Jesus and those well-known, mighty Christians who have strived for God in effort and prayer. When we learn to come to God with an intense desire that grips the soul, then we will know the power in prayer greater than what we know now.

But how shall we get to this place of earnest prayer?

Not by trying to work ourselves up into it. The true method is explained in Rom. 8:26, *"Likewise the Spirit helps us in our weakness. For we do not know what to pray for as we ought, but the Spirit himself intercedes for us with groanings too deep for words."* The earnestness that we work up in the energy of the flesh is a disgusting thing. The earnestness worked in us by the power of the Holy Spirit is pleasing to God. If we want to pray correctly, we must look to the Spirit of God to teach us to pray.

This is where fasting comes in. In Dan. 9:3, we read that Daniel set his face *"to the Lord God, seeking him by prayer and pleas for mercy with fasting and sackcloth and ashes."* Some think that fasting belongs to the old way of things; but when we look at Acts 14:23, and Acts 13:2,3, we find that it was very much a part of earnest men at that time.

If we would pray with power, we should pray with fasting. This of course does not mean that we should fast every time we pray. However, there are times of emergency or special crisis in work or in our individual lives, when earnest Christians will deny their natural appetites so that they may give themselves up completely to prayer.

There is exceptional power in such prayer. Every great crisis in life and work should be met in that way. God is not pleased with us giving up things like a Pharisee or in a legalistic manner. But there is power in that earnestness and determination to obtain the things of which we desperately need in prayer. This is what leads us to put away everything, even the things that are necessary and right, that we may set our faces to find God, and gain the blessings He has for us.

By The Church

Again we look to verse, Acts 12:5 for the third way to ensure powerful prayer. It appears in the three words *"by the church."*

There is power in *united prayer*. Of course, there is power in the prayer of an individual, but it is increased in united prayer. God delights in the unity of His people and seeks to emphasize it in every way. And so He gives a special blessing on united prayer. In Matthew 18:19 it says, *"If two of you agree on earth about anything they ask, it will be done for them by my Father in heaven."*

This unity, however, must be real. The passage just quoted does not say that if two shall agree in asking. Two people might agree to ask for the same thing, and yet there is no real agreement in the Spirit. One might ask because he desired it, the other might ask it simply to please his friend. But where there is a real agreement, where the Spirit of God brings two believers into perfect harmony and lays the same burden on their hearts; that prayer is filled with overwhelming power.

Study Questions

Whether you are alone or in a group, these questions can be used as starting points. Use them to think about further questions you may have, to find other verses in the Bible that say the same thing, or to open up a deeper discussion with others.

You don't have to answer each question and can skip some, or stay on just one— as long as you are challenged to think more about what has been said.

1. What is the difference between "from God" and "to God," when we are talking about prayer?
2. Torrey says we should not be quick with our words when praying. What does this mean?
3. What does "without ceasing" mean in prayer? Do you think it's possible?
4. Torrey mentions the "rest of faith" and the "fight of faith." What is the difference?
5. What do you understand about fasting? Is there a place for it in our lives today?

6. Have you ever experienced unity in prayer with other believers; or do you often just agree with what they are asking for?
7. Is it possible to be truly united with other Christians when praying? How?

3

OBEYING AND PRAYING

Whatever He Asks

One of the most significant verses in the Bible on prayer is 1 John 3:22. John says, *"And whatever we ask we receive from him, because we keep his commandments and do what pleases him."*

What a statement! John says that everything he asked for he received. How many of us can say this: "Whatever I ask for I receive"? But John explains why. *"Because we keep His commandments, and do what pleases him."* In other words, the one who expects God to do as he asks Him, must play his part and do whatever God asks of him.

If we listen to all God's commands us to do, He will listen to all our requests to Him. However, if we don't want to hear His direction, He will not hear our prayers. This is the secret to many of our unanswered prayers. We are not listening to God's Word, and so He is not listening to our petitions.

I spoke with a woman who had been a Christian, but then gave it all up. I asked her why she was not a Christian anymore. She said it was because she did not believe the Bible. I asked her why she did not believe the Bible.

"Because I have tried its promises and found them untrue."

"Which promises?"

"The promises about prayer."

"Which promises about prayer?"

"Does it not say in the Bible, 'Whatever you ask, believing you shall receive?'"

"It says something like that."

"Well, I asked fully expecting to get and did not receive, so the promise failed."

"Was the promise made to you?"

"Isn't it made for all Christians?"

"No, God carefully defines the word 'you' in this verse, Who they are. Whose believing prayers He agrees to answer."

I then turned her to 1 John 3:22 and read the description of those people whose prayers had power with God.

"Now," I said, "were you keeping His commandments and doing those things which are pleasing in His sight?"

She confessed that she was not, and soon came to see that the real difficulty was not with God's promises, but with herself. That is the difficulty with many unanswered prayers today: The one who offers it is not obedient.

If we would have power in prayer, we must be diligent students of His Word to find out what His will for our lives is, and then do it. One unconfessed act of disobedience will shut the ear of God against many prayers.

What Pleases Him

But this verse goes beyond simply keeping God's commandments. John tells us that we must do what pleases Him.

There are many things God has not actually commanded us to do. Still, when we do those things, He is greatly pleased. A true child is not just happy doing what his father tells him to do. He wants to know his father's will, and if he thinks that there is anything he can do that would please his father, he gladly does it— even though he was never asked to do it. It's the same with the true child of God. He does not only ask what is instructed and what is prohibited but studies to know his Father's will in all things.

There are many Christians today who are doing things that are not pleasing to God and leaving things that would be pleasing to God undone. When you speak to them about these things they will confront you with the question, "Does the Bible tell us anywhere that we cannot do this thing?" And if you can't show them a verse showing that thing is clearly forbidden, they think they are under no obligation to give it up.

A true child of God does not need a specific command. If we desire to find and do the things that are pleasing to God, He will do the things that are pleasing to us. This gives us another explanation for many unanswered prayers: We are not concerned with knowing what would please our Father, and so our prayers are not answered.

An example of this is the many questions that are always asked about dancing, smoking, and questionable movies. Those people who do these things will proudly ask if you are against them, "Does the Bible say, 'Thou shalt not go watch that movie?'" "Does the Bible say, 'Thou shalt not dance'?" "Does the Bible say, 'Thou shalt not smoke'?" That is not the question. The question is: Is our heavenly Father pleased when He sees one of His children watching that, dancing like that, or smoking? That is a question we must each decide for ourselves, prayerfully, seeking guidance from the Holy Spirit. Many ask, "Where is the harm in these things?" There isn't time to spend answering this question, except to state the obvious; they rob our prayers of power.

In Truth

Psalm 145:18 helps us to answer the question of how to pray: *"The Lord is near to all who call on him, to all who call on him in truth."*

The phrase, *"in truth"* needs a closer look. In a concordance, you will see that it means "in reality" or "in sincerity." The prayer that God answers is the prayer that is real, the prayer that asks for something that is sincerely desired.

Most prayers are insincere. People ask for things that they do not wish for. Many women are praying for their husbands to be born again, but they don't really want that to happen. They think they do, but if they knew what would be involved in the husband coming to Jesus, how it would completely change the way he did business, and how his income might be impacted resulting in different living standards, the real prayer of her heart would be different. If the wife was really sincere with God, she would say:

"O God, do not convert my husband."

The cost is too great.

Many churches are praying for a revival, but do not really desire a revival. They think they do, because to them a revival means more people on Sunday, an increase in tithes, and a better reputation among other churches. But if they knew what a real revival meant, how those Christians involved would need to search their hearts, the radical transformation of the individual, domestic and social lives that would take place, and many other things that would happen if the Spirit of God was properly poured out, then the prayer would be different. If they were honest, the real cry of the church would be:

"O God, keep us from having a revival."

Many ministers are praying for the baptism of the Holy Spirit, but do not really want it. They think they do because to them it means a new joy, a new power in preaching, a wider reputation, and a greater role in the church. But if they understood what it really involved, how it would cause friction between them and the world, and with unspiritual Christians, how it would cause their reputations to suffer, even mean some need to leave good comfortable lives to go work in the slums, or even in a foreign land, then they might not pray this. If they understood all this, the real wish of their hearts would be:

"O God, save me from being baptized with the Holy Spirit."

But when we do come to the place where we desire the conversion of friends at any cost, really desire the outpouring of the Holy Spirit whatever it may involve, really desire the baptism with the Holy Spirit regardless of the consequences, where we desire anything *"in truth;"* and only then call upon God for it "in truth" God is going to hear.

Study Questions

Obedience is a key aspect of Christianity, and many of us simply end up doing things because we have to. This chapter challenges that idea. Take some time to look at your own life and to see areas where you do things out of obligation rather than to please God.

This may be hard to admit, but this is where we grow—admitting our weaknesses and failures and allowing God to lead us forward.

If you are brave enough, take the next step and share these things with someone else. It's a good way to be held accountable so that it is not merely self-reflection, but a challenge to deal with those things.

1. What are God's commandments for us as Christians? (refer to Gal. 5:14)
2. What is God's will for our lives? Is it the same as his commandments?
3. What do you think pleases God the most?
4. Torrey says "A true child of God does not need a specific command." What do you make of this statement?
5. Praying in truth means looking at the real motives of what we are asking for. Think about the last few things you have prayed for, what were your motives behind those?
6. Compare praying in truth to what Jesus says to the woman at the well in John 4:24.
7. What is meant by obedience is better than sacrifice in 1 Samuel 15:22?

4

PRAYING IN JESUS' NAME ACCORDING TO GOD'S WILL

In His Name

On the night before His crucifixion, Jesus said these amazing words to the disciples: *"Whatever you ask in my name, this I will do, that the Father may be glorified in the Son ... If you ask me anything in my name, I will do it,"* (John 16:23, John 14:14).

Prayer in Jesus' name has power with God. God is pleased with His Son, and He always hears Him. He also always hears every prayer that is in His name. There is a fragrance in the name of Christ that makes these prayers acceptable to God.

What does it mean to pray in Jesus' name?

Many have tried to explain this but often made it too complicated. There is nothing mysterious about it. If we look at all the verses in the Bible with the phrases, "in My name" or "in His name," we will find that it means exactly the same as it means to us today.

If I go to a bank and hand in a check with my name signed on it, I am asking the bank for money *in my own name*. If I have money at that bank, I will be paid; if not, then the check is worthless. However, if I go to the bank with somebody else's name signed on the check, I am asking *in his name*. It does not matter if I have money in that bank or not, if the person whose name is on the check has money there, I will be paid out.

For example, if I went to the bank with a check that I had signed for $50, the teller would say, "Mr. Torrey, we cannot cash that. You have no money in this bank." But if I went to the same bank with a check for $5,000 made out to me, and signed by one of the large depositors in that bank, they would not ask if I had money in that bank or any bank but would cash the check and give me the $5000 at once.

It is the same when I go to the bank of heaven when I go to God in prayer. I have nothing deposited there, I have absolutely no credit there, and if I go in my own name I will get absolutely nothing. But Jesus Christ has unlimited credit in heaven, and He has granted to me the privilege of going to the bank with His name on my checks. When I go in His name, my prayers will be honored.

To pray in Jesus' name is to pray on His credit— not mine. It is letting go of any claims I have on God and approaching Him on His claims. It is not simply adding "I ask these things in Jesus' name" to my prayer. I say it but rely on my strength. When I come to God, not on my strength, but on Jesus' strength. Not on my goodness, but through the atoning blood (Heb. 10:19), God will hear me. Much of our prayer is useless because we imagine we have some sort of claim on God and that He is under an obligation to answer our prayers.

Years ago when Mr. Moody first began in the ministry, he visited a town in Illinois. There was a judge there who was an atheist, and so his wife asked Mr. Moody to visit her husband.

Mr. Moody replied, "I cannot talk with your husband. I am only a young, uneducated Christian, and your husband is an atheist."

The wife would not take no for an answer, so Mr. Moody visited the judge. Those working in the office laughed to themselves as they saw the young salesman from Chicago go in to talk with the academic judge.

The conversation was short.

Mr. Moody said, "Judge, I can't talk with you. You are an educated atheist, and I have no learning, but I simply want to say if you are ever converted, I want you to let me know."

The judge replied, "Yes, young man, if I am ever converted I will let you know."

The conversation ended. The office workers laughed, even more, when the enthusiastic, young Christian left. But in less than a year, the judge was born again. Mr. Moody visited again and asked the judge what had happened.

The judge said, "One night, when my wife was at a prayer meeting, I grew uneasy and miserable. I didn't know what was wrong with me but finally went to bed before she came home. I could not sleep all that night. I got up early, told my wife that I would skip breakfast, and went to work. I told my staff to take the day off, and shut myself in my office."

"I grew even more miserable, and finally I got down and asked God to forgive my sins, but I would not say 'for Jesus' sake,' because I didn't believe in salvation. I kept praying 'God forgive my sins,' but there was no answer. At last, in desperation I cried, 'O God, for Christ's sake forgive my sins,' and I immediately felt peace."

The judge had no access to God until he came in the name of Christ. When he finally did, he was heard and immediately answered.

In Confidence

If we want to know how to truly pray, then 1 John 5:14-15 shows us an answer: *"And this is the confidence that we have toward him, that if we ask anything according to his will he hears us. And if we know that he hears us in whatever we ask, we know that we have the requests that we have asked of him."*

It teaches us that if we are to pray correctly, we must pray according to God's will, then we can be certain that we will get what we ask of Him.

But can we know the will of God? Can we know that any specific prayer is according to His will?

Yes, we can.

How?

By The Word

God has revealed His will in His Word. When anything is promised in the Word of God, we know that it is His will to give that thing. So when I pray and put a promise from the Bible before God, I know that He hears me. And if I know He hears me, I know that I have what I have asked of Him.

For example, when I pray for wisdom, I know it is God's will to give me wisdom. He says in James 1:5: *"If any of you lacks wisdom, let him ask God, who gives generously to all without reproach, and it will be given him."* So when I ask for wisdom, I know that the prayer is heard, and that wisdom will be given to me.

When I pray for the Holy Spirit, I know from Luke 11:13 that it is God's will that my prayer is heard, and that I have received what I asked for: *"If you then, who are evil, know how to give good gifts to your children, how much more will the heavenly Father give the Holy Spirit to those who ask him!"*

Once, a minister came to me at the end of a sermon on prayer at a Y.M.C.A. Bible school said, "You have given those young men the impression that they can ask for specific things and get exactly what they ask for."

I replied that I was not sure if that was the impression I had given, but it was certainly the impression that I wanted to give.

"But," he replied, "that is not right. We can't be sure, for we don't know God's will."

I opened to James 1:5, read it, and said to him, "Is it not God's will to give us wisdom, and if you ask for wisdom do you not know that you are going to get it?"

"Ah!" he said, "we don't know what wisdom is."

I said, "No, if we did, we would not need to ask. But whatever wisdom may be, don't you know that you will get it?"

It is our privilege to know. When we have a specific promise in the Word of God, if we doubt that it is God's will, or if we doubt that God will do the thing that we ask, we make God a liar.

This is one of the greatest secrets of successful prayer: To study the Bible and see what God's will is as shown in His promises. Then to simply take these promises and spread them out before God in prayer with the expectation that He will do what He has promised in His Word.

By The Spirit

There is another way we can know the will of God: By the teaching of His Holy Spirit.

There are many things we need from God that are not in any of the specific promises in the Bible, but even in those situations, we can know what His will is.

In Rom. 8:26-27, we are told, *"Likewise the Spirit helps us in our weakness. For we do not know what to pray for as we ought, but the Spirit himself intercedes for us with groanings too deep for words. And he who searches hearts knows what is the mind of the Spirit, because the Spirit intercedes for the saints <u>according to the will of God</u>."*

It is clear that the Spirit of God prays in us and draws out our prayer in line with God's will. If we are led by the Holy Spirit to pray for something, we can do so knowing it is God's will; and that we will receive it, even though the Bible doesn't specifically promise it.

Often God through the Holy Spirit lays it on our hearts to pray for someone. We cannot rest, we pray for that person with groanings too deep for words. Maybe we cannot reach them ourselves, but God hears the prayer, and soon we hear they have been born again.

1 John 5:14-15 is one of the most abused passages in the Bible: *"And this is <u>the confidence</u> that we have toward him, that if we ask anything according to his will he hears us. And if we know that he hears us in whatever we ask, we know that we have the requests that we have asked of him."*

This was added into the Bible by the Holy Spirit to encourage our faith. It begins with *"This is <u>the confidence</u> that we have toward him,"* and closes with *"<u>we know</u> that we have the requests that we have asked of him."* But instead of producing confidence, this passage has been used to bring uncertainty into our prayers.

When someone prays confidently, some cautious person will say, "Now, don't be too confident. If it is God's will He will do it. You should put in, 'If it is Your will.'"

Of course, there are many times we don't know the will of God, and as we pray we should be submitting to His will anyway. However, when we know God's will, we don't need any "ifs." This passage was not put into the Bible so we could introduce "ifs" into our prayers, but so that we might throw our "ifs" to the wind— have *"confidence"* and *"know that we have the requests that we have asked of Him."*

Study Questions

Don't rush through these questions. Take your time. You can even spend an hour or a day on just one as you need time to reflect, think, and do some Bible study on it. This way it can take root, going past our initial, quick answers that we often give, and reveal more of what God wants to show us about prayer— about our own lives.

1. Is it important to use the actual phrase, "in Jesus' name" when we pray?
2. The analogy of cashing a cheque at a bank is used to show what it means to pray in Jesus' name. What do you understand about this?
3. Is praying loudly and boldly the same as praying confidently?
4. Do you know any other promises found in the Bible? Look at them, thinking about what Torrey says about praying by the Word.

5. There is a lot of talk about the Holy Spirit in this book. Have you ever prayed, allowing the Spirit to help you in your prayers?
6. Do you pray confidently or cautiously? Look at 1 John 5:14-15 as you respond.
7. Which one do you find easier: To pray by the Word or in the Spirit?

5

PRAYING IN THE SPIRIT

In The Spirit

Over and over we see our dependence on the Holy Spirit in prayer. It's very clear in Ephesians 6:18, *"praying at all times in the Spirit,"* and in Jude 20, *"praying in the Holy Spirit."* The whole secret of prayer is found in these three words, "in the Spirit." The prayer that God the Father answers is the one inspired by God the Holy Spirit.

The disciples didn't know how to pray, so they asked Jesus to teach them. We also don't know how to pray properly, but we have a Teacher and Guide to help us (John 14:16-17), *"the Spirit helps us in our weakness."* (Rom. 8:26). He teaches us how to pray. True prayer is prayer in the Spirit-inspired and directed by Him.

When we come into God's presence we should recognize "our weakness"— our ignorance of what to pray for and how to pray for it. Knowing this, we can look to the Holy Spirit, asking Him to guide our prayers; to help us with the words and the direction.

It is not clever to rush into God's presence and ask the first thing that comes into our mind or something a friend has asked us to pray for. When we come into God's presence, we should first be silent before Him. We must wait for the Holy Spirit, and surrender ourselves to the Spirit, then we shall pray correctly.

Often we do not feel like praying. What should we do then? Stop until we feel like it? No. When we don't feel like praying is when we need to pray the most. We should wait quietly before God and tell Him how cold and prayerless our hearts are. We need to look to Him. Trust and expect Him to send the Holy Spirit to warm our hearts and draw them into prayer. It will not be long before the glow of the Spirit's presence fills our hearts, and we can pray with freedom, directness, earnestness, and power.

Many of the most wonderful prayer times I have known began with a feeling of complete deadness and prayerlessness. But in my helplessness and coldness, I brought myself before God and looked to Him to send His Holy Spirit to teach me to pray— and He has done it.

When we pray in the Spirit, we will pray for the right things and in the right way. There will be joy and power in our prayer.

With Faith

If we are to pray with the power we must pray with faith. In Mark 11:24 Jesus says, *"Therefore I tell you, whatever you ask in prayer, believe that you have received it, and it will be yours."*

No matter how positive the promises in the Bible are, we will not enjoy them unless we confidently expect them to happen in answer to our prayer. James 1:5 says, *"If any of you lacks wisdom let him ask God, who gives generously to all without reproach, and it will be given him."* Now that promise is as positive as a promise can be.

But verse 6-7 adds, *"But let him ask in faith, with no doubting, for the one who doubts is like a wave of the sea that is driven and tossed by the wind. For that person must not suppose that he will receive anything from the Lord."* There needs to be a confident expectation. But there is a faith that goes beyond expectation, that believes that the prayer is heard and the promise granted. We can see this in Mark 11:24, *"Therefore I tell you, whatever you ask in prayer, believe that you have received it, and it will be yours."*

How can we get this faith?

It cannot be pumped up. Many of us read this promise about the prayer of faith, and then ask for whatever we desire while trying to make ourselves believe that God has heard the prayer. We only end up disappointed. This is not real faith; so what we asked for is not given. At this point, many people have a total collapse of faith. Trying to build up faith through their effort and willpower and receiving nothing in response can cause the whole foundation of their faith to crumble.

How does real faith come?

Romans 10:17 answers the question: *"So faith comes from hearing, and hearing through the word of Christ."* Real faith comes from studying the Bible and finding out what is promised, then simply believing God's promises. Faith must have a guarantee. Trying to believe something that you want to believe is not faith. Believing what God says in His Word is faith.

To have faith when I pray, I must find some promise in the Bible on which to rest my faith. Faith then comes through the Spirit. The Spirit knows the will of God, and if I pray in the Spirit, and look to the Spirit to teach me God's will, He will lead me in line with that will and give me faith that the prayer will be answered. But real faith never comes by just deciding that you are going to receive what you want.

If there is no promise in the Bible and no clear leading of the Spirit, there can be no real faith. In such a case, no one can blame a person for lacking faith. But if the thing we desire is promised in the Bible, we can only criticize ourselves for not having faith if we doubt— we are making God a liar by doubting His Word.

Study Questions

Many churches and Christians differ in their response to where the Holy Spirit fits, what He can do, and what His work in our lives today should be. Using verses, Torrey explains that He is very active and very necessary in our lives today— especially in prayer.

These questions may seem controversial if you don't agree with what this book says about them. Instead of rejecting these ideas, explore them and search the Bible for answers.

1. John 16:7 uses the term, Helper when talking about the Holy Spirit. Why?
2. Waiting for the Spirit to guide you in prayer can be difficult for us. What do you think makes it like that?
3. What should we do when we don't feel like praying?
4. What is your definition of faith? (see Heb. 11:1).
5. Do you ever doubt that God will actually come through when you pray?
6. If we don't have any faith, how can we get it?
7. How do you think faith and the Holy Spirit are connected?

6

ALWAYS PRAYING AND NOT GIVING UP

There are two parables in Luke that Jesus uses to teach us that we should always pray and not give up.

The first parable:

"And he said to them, "Which of you who has a friend will go to him at midnight and say to him, 'Friend, lend me three loaves, for a friend of mine has arrived on a journey, and I have nothing to set before him; and he will answer from within, 'Do not bother me; the door is now shut, and my children are with me in bed. I cannot get up and give you anything? I tell you, though he will not get up and give him anything because he is his friend, yet because of his impudence he will rise and give him whatever he needs," (Luke 11:5-8).

The second parable:

"And he told them a parable to the effect that they ought always to pray and not lose heart. He said, "In a certain city there was a judge who neither feared God nor respected man. And there was a widow

in that city who kept coming to him and saying, 'Give me justice against my adversary.' For a while he refused, but afterward he said to himself, 'Though I neither fear God nor respect man, yet because this widow keeps bothering me, I will give her justice, so that she will not beat me down by her continual coming.'" And the Lord said, *"Hear what the unrighteous judge says. And will not God give justice to his elect, who cry to him day and night? Will he delay long over them? I tell you, he will give justice to them speedily. Nevertheless, when the Son of Man comes, will he find faith on earth?"* (Luke 18:1-8).

In the first parables, Jesus outlines the need for persistence in prayer. The word rendered "impudence"— literally means "shamelessness" or "audacity." Jesus wants to show us that when we come to God to ask for something, we should have a determination that feels no shame if we are refused or there is a delay. God delights in the holy boldness that will not take "no" for an answer. It is a show of great faith, and nothing pleases God more than faith.

When the Canaanite woman comes to Jesus to heal her daughter, it seems as though he brushes her off very rudely, but she does not back down. Jesus looked upon her shameless persistence with pleasure, and said, *"O woman, great is your faith! Be it done for you as you desire."* (Matt. 15:28) God does not always just give us what we want on our first effort. He wants to train us and make us stronger by pushing us to work hard for the best things. He makes us *pray through*.

I am happy about this because there is no greater training in prayer than being pressured to ask again and again and again, even over many years before we get what we ask for from

God. Some call it submitting to God's will when He doesn't grant them their requests after asking once or twice.

They say, "Well, maybe it's not God's will."

This is not submission, but spiritual laziness. Submitting to God's will is not giving up after a couple of efforts— this is just a weakness of character. When a strong man sets out to do something, and he does not get it right the first attempt, or the second, or one-hundredth time; he keeps hammering away until he does accomplish it. The strong man of prayer keeps on praying until he prays it through, and obtains what he seeks. We must be careful about what we ask from God. But if it is something in line with His will, then once we start to pray, we should never give up until we get it, or until God makes it very clear that it is not His will to give it.

Some people argue that it shows unbelief to pray twice for the same thing and say that we should "take it" the first time we ask. There are times through faith in the Word or the leading of the Holy Spirit where we can *claim* what we have asked of God after just one prayer. But there is no doubt that there are other times when we must pray again and again and again for the same thing before we get our answer.

Those of us who have gone beyond just praying two or three times for the same thing have gone further than their Master did in the garden, (Matthew 26:44). George Muller prayed for two men every day for almost sixty years. One of them was born again just before Muller died, and the other shortly after his death. We need men and women who will not just start praying for things, but carry on and on and on until they get what they ask from the Lord.

Study Questions

If you have a notebook or some paper, it will help to write down your answers to these questions, your thoughts on the passages, or even verses connected with them. This is a great way to study and reflect on issues such as prayer. By doing this, you can go back at a later stage and compare what you thought to what you know now. Often we will be surprised at the growth we see in our own lives.

Take time, to be honest in these questions— write down your answers.

1. Are you the type of person who pursues something until they get there? Are you the same in your prayer life?
2. Do you think it's possible to be timid and gentle as a person, but tenacious in prayer? (see 2 Tim. 1:7)
3. Torrey used the phrase, "pray through" often during his life. What does it mean?
4. Is 'Naming and Claiming' something the same as having faith in prayer for it?
5. Why do you think God sometimes answers immediately, and other times He doesn't?
6. Why does Torrey make the distinction between submission and weakness?
7. Have you ever prayed for something more than once? What happened?

7
ABIDING IN JESUS

"*If you abide in me, and my words abide in you, ask whatever you wish, and it will be done for you.*" (John 15:7) The whole secret of prayer is found in these words that Jesus said. This is prayer with incredible power: "*ask <u>whatever you wish</u>, and it will be done for you.*"

There is a way to ask and get exactly what we ask. Jesus gives us two conditions:

Abide In Me

The first condition is, "If you abide in me."

What does it mean to abide in Christ?

Some explanations are so spiritual or so deep that to most of us ordinary Christians they don't mean much at all. But what Jesus meant was very simple.

He was comparing Himself to a vine, and His disciples to the branches in that vine. Some branches remained and lived in the vine so that its sap or life constantly flowed into them. They had no independent life of their own. Everything in them was the overflow of the vine's life in them. Their buds, leaves, blossoms, and fruit were not theirs alone but belong to the vine.

Other branches were either completely cut off from the vine, or the sap or life of the vine was blocked somehow.

For us to abide in Christ is to have the same relationship as the first branches to the vine. That means giving up our own independent life; our thoughts, resolutions, and feelings, and looking always to Jesus to think His thoughts in us, form His purposes in us, and feel His emotions in us. It is surrendering all life that is independent of Christ and looking to Him to pour His life into us and work His life through us. When we do this, our prayers will find what we want from God.

Of course, our desires won't be ours, but His. Our prayers won't be ours, but Jesus praying in us. These prayers will always be in line with God's will, and the Father always hears Him. When our prayers fail it is because they are our prayers, not His. The desire and request have come from us, instead of Jesus praying through us.

To abide in Christ, praying through Him rather than ourselves, is simply saying we are praying "in the Spirit." Abiding in Christ means our thoughts, our joys, and our fruit are not our own, but His. The same way the buds, leaves, blossoms, and fruit are not from the branch, but from the vine whose life is flowing into the branch and manifesting itself in these buds, leaves, blossoms, and fruit.

Abiding in Jesus means we have already accepted Him as our Savior, He has saved us from our sin, and is Lord of our lives. Being in Jesus, all we have to do to abide (or continue) in Him is to give up our self-life. That means surrendering every thought, purpose, desire, and affection of our own, and looking to Jesus every day to form His thoughts, purposes, affections, and desires in us. Abiding in Christ is really very simple and is a wonderful life of privilege and power.

My Words Abide In You

In John 15:7, there is another condition, but it is connected to the first one: "And My words abide in you."

If we want to receive all that we ask from God, Jesus' words must abide or continue in us. We must study His words, meditate on them, let them sink into our thoughts and our heart. Memorize them, obey them, let them shape and guide our daily lives and actions.

This is how we abide in Christ: Through His words, Jesus imparts Himself to us. The words He speaks are spirit and life. (John 6:33) It is useless to expect power in prayer unless we meditate on Jesus' words, letting them sink deep into our hearts. Many people wonder why their prayers are so weak, but it is because they have not hidden His words in their hearts; His words do not abide in them. It is not through incredible, supernatural meditation and experiences that we learn to abide in Christ.

Instead, it's by feeding on His words in the Bible and allowing the Holy Spirit to plant them in our hearts and to make them grow. If we do this, Jesus' words will motivate us to pray. They will be the mold in which our prayers are shaped, in line with God's will. Successful prayer is almost impossible when we ignore studying God's Word.

Studying the Bible academically is not enough; we have to meditate on it. We must consider each word, letting the Spirit make them come alive in our hearts. A prayer that comes from spending time meditating on the Word will go straight to God's ears.

George Muller, a mighty man of prayer, would start by reading and meditating on God's Word until a prayer began to form in his heart. God was the real author of that prayer. And so God answered those prayers that were inspired by Him.

The Word of God is the instrument through which the Holy Spirit works— it is the sword of the Spirit. If we want to know the work of the Holy Spirit in any direction, we must feed on the Word. If we want to pray in the Spirit, we must meditate on the Bible, so that the Holy Spirit may have something to work through. Without the Word, this cannot happen. If we feed the fire of our prayers with the fuel of God's Word, all our difficulties in prayer would disappear.

Study Questions

As Christians, we may have come across the word, 'abide' quite often. It literally means to live in, remain, endure, obey, or accept. Go through this chapter again, and substitute each of these words (or other synonyms) every time you see 'abide.' It may help you to understand this chapter a bit more.

Next go through these study questions with this picture of the phrase, 'abide in Me' in your mind. As you do, ask yourself how much you abide in Jesus.

1. In your own words, what does it mean to abide in Christ? (see 1 John 2:28, Gal 2:20, 1 John 2:6, 2 Cor 5:17)
2. Would abiding in Christ change the way we pray?
3. What are the benefits of abiding in Jesus?
4. Surrendering to God is also a common phrase used. Is there any connection with abiding in Jesus?
5. What is the connection between prayer and the Word?
6. Have you ever made reading the Bible a part of your time in prayer? Do you think it would benefit your prayers at all?
7. Now, look back at the key verse of John 15:7. How does what you have understood about abiding in Jesus and His Word in you, change the phrase, "whatever you wish"?

8
PRAY WITH THANKSGIVING

We often miss two words from Paul's lesson about prayer in Philippians 4:6-7, *"Do not be anxious about anything, but in everything by prayer and supplication with thanksgiving let your requests be made known to God. And the peace of God, which surpasses all understanding, will guard your hearts and your minds in Christ Jesus."*

The two important words we miss are, *"with thanksgiving."*

When we ask God for blessings, we must not forget to thank Him for all the blessings He has already given us. If we stop to think how many of our prayers He has answered and how we hardly give thanks for them, I am sure we would be shocked. Our thanks should be as clear as our prayers. We can come with very specific requests, but our thanksgiving is often vague.

One reason why so many of our prayers are weak is that we haven't given thanks for the blessings we have received. If someone always came asking us to help them, but they never said, "Thank you," we would get tired of helping such an ungrateful person. Sometimes our heavenly Father is wise enough to refuse to answer our prayers so that we can be taught to be thankful.

God is saddened by the thanklessness and ingratitude that so many of us are guilty of. When Jesus healed the ten lepers and only one came back to thank Him, He was surprised and hurt enough to say, *"Were not ten cleansed? Where are the nine?"* (Luke 17:17).

God must be so sad when He looks down at how we forget all of His blessings and answers to our prayers.

Giving thanks for blessings increases our faith and allows us to come to God with new confidence. The reason people have so little faith when they pray is that they take so little time to meditate on and thank God for blessings already received. As we think on the answers to prayers we have got, faith grows bolder; we can feel in our hearts that there is nothing too hard for the Lord. As we reflect upon the goodness of God, as well as how little time and effort we put into thanksgiving, we can only be humble enough to confess our sin.

The mighty men of prayer in the Bible and the history of the church have been men who gave thanksgiving and praise. David was a mighty man of prayer. His Psalms are filled with thanksgiving and praise. The apostles were mighty men of prayer; we read that they *"were continually in the temple blessing God,"* (Luke 24:53). Paul was a mighty man of prayer, and his letters are crammed with specific thanksgiving to God for specific blessings and answers to prayers.

Jesus is our model in prayer and everything else. When we study His life we find that when he gave thanks for the simplest meal after His resurrection, it was so evident that this is how the two disciples recognized Him.

Thanksgiving is one of the inevitable results of being filled with the Holy Spirit and a person who does not learn to *"give thanks in all circumstances,"* (1 Thess 5:18), cannot continue to pray in the Spirit. If we want to learn to pray with the power we must let these two words sink deep into our hearts: *"with thanksgiving."*

Study Questions

This chapter on thanksgiving is another aspect we know much about but that many of us practice so little. Once again, be vulnerable in your answers, even if it exposes insecurity and weaknesses. This book is not to condemn you, but to encourage and challenge you so you can see if you are lacking in any area— or become more mature.

After you have gone through these questions, if you are in a group, you can begin to discuss the many things God has done for you. It can be a time of sharing testimonies of times in your life that He has answered prayer or come through for you without you even asking. In doing this, you will be expressing your gratitude to Him.

1. How often do you ask God for things? How often do you thank Him for those same things He has given to you?
2. Are you naturally a grateful person, or do you have to work hard at it?
3. Do you think it's possible for God to be saddened when we forget to thank Him?
4. Torrey makes a very harsh statement that someone who cannot give thanks in all circumstances, cannot carry on praying in the Spirit. What do you think of this?
5. Read 1 Thess. 5:16-18. Go over each part and ask yourself if you do these, or not.
6. Torrey says that thanksgiving is inevitable if you are filled with the Holy Spirit. What does this mean?
7. Make a list of everything you can think of that you are thankful to God for.

9
OBSTACLES TO PRAYER

We have looked at all the positive requirements of prayer, but some things restrict prayer. God has made these very clear.

Your Own Desires

The first obstacle we find in James 4:3, *"You ask and do not receive, because you ask wrongly, to spend it on your passions."*

A selfish purpose robs prayer of its power. Most prayers are selfish. It may be perfectly alright to ask for things that are God's will to give us, but our motives are completely wrong, so that prayer is not effective. The true purpose in prayer is that God may be glorified in the answer. If we ask for something only to use it for our own pleasure, we "ask wrongly" — therefore shouldn't expect to receive it. This explains why many prayers are unanswered.

For example, a woman praying for her husband to be born again is a good thing to ask for. But her motive in asking for that is selfish because she desires to have a husband who sympathizes with her or doesn't want to think that he might die and be lost forever. The prayer is purely selfish. Why should a woman desire the conversion of her husband? First, that God may be glorified. She should be more concerned that God is dishonored by her husband completely ignoring Jesus.

Many pray for a revival. That is pleasing to God and is in line with His will. But many prayers for revivals are purely selfish. Churches desire revivals so that the number of members can grow, the church may have more influence in the community, the church finances may increase, and the church council can receive a glowing report of how well the church is doing. Often, God doesn't answer prayers like these that have such low expectations.

Then why should we pray for a revival? For the glory of God!

We should not be able to stand by while God is dishonored by the worldliness of the church, by the sins of unbelievers, the proud unbelief that exists, and because the Bible is ignored. It should be our desire that He is glorified by His Spirit being poured into the church. These are the reasons we should pray for a revival.

Many prayers for the Holy Spirit are purely selfish.

It is God's will to give the Holy Spirit to everyone that asks—He has said so (Luke 11:13). But many of these prayers are blocked by the selfish motives behind them. Men and women pray for the Holy Spirit so that they may be happy, don't experience defeat in their lives, have power as Christian workers, or have some other selfish motive. Why should we pray for the Spirit? So that God may not be dishonored by our weak Christianity and unproductive service, and that He may be glorified in the beauty and power that comes to our lives and service.

Our Sins

The second obstacle to prayer is found in Isaiah 59:1-2: *"Behold, the Lord's hand is not shortened, that it cannot save, or his ear dull, that it cannot hear; but your iniquities have made a separation between you and your God, and your sins have hidden his face from you so that he does not hear."*

Sin stops prayer. We can pray and pray and pray, and get absolutely no answer to our prayers. We might think that it's not God's will to answer, or that He no longer answers prayers as He did. The Israelites thought the same thing, that the Lord's hand was too short to save, and His ear too dull to hear them.

"Not so," said Isaiah, "God's ear is just as open to hearing as ever. His hand is just as mighty to save. But there is a barrier: Your own sins. They have separated you from your God, and have hidden His face so that He will not hear."

It is the same today. Our cries to God are in vain, because of sin in our lives. It could be some past sin that has not been confessed and dealt with or a sin that we enjoy holding onto, even to think it is not a sin. Where sin is hidden in our hearts and lives, God "will not hear."

If our prayers are not working, instead of wondering if it is in line with His will or not, we should rather come to God with the Psalmist's prayer, *"Search me, O God, and know my heart! Try me and know my thoughts! And see if there be any grievous way in me,"* (Ps. 139:23-24). We should wait before Him until He puts His finger on whatever it is that offends Him; then confess and deal with it immediately.

I remember a time when I was praying for two specific things that I needed, but the answer didn't come. I woke up in the middle of the night suffering in my body and my heart. I cried to God for the things I wanted, explaining how necessary they were to me, but no answer came. Then I asked Him to show me if there was anything wrong in my life. Something popped into my mind that I had thought of a few times before, but had not seen as a sin.

I said to God, "If this is wrong I will give it up." Still, no answer came. In my heart, I knew the thing was wrong.

At last, I said, "This *is* wrong. I have sinned. I will give it up."

Peace filled me, and I was soon sleeping like a child. In the morning I woke up feeling well, and the money that I needed to do the work that would honor God's name came.

Sin is an awful thing. One of the most awful things about it is how it blocks prayer and cuts us off from grace, power, and blessing. If we want power in our prayer we must not tolerate any sin in our lives. *"If I had cherished iniquity in my heart, the Lord would not have listened."* (Psalms 66:18) If we hold on to sin or anything between us and God, we cannot expect Him to listen to our prayers. Anything that constantly comes up while you are spending time with God is the thing that stops prayer— put it away.

Idols Of The Heart

Next, we look to Ezekiel 14:3, *"Son of man, these men have taken their <u>idols into their hearts</u>, and set the stumbling block of their iniquity before their faces. Should I indeed let myself be consulted by them?"*

God refuses to answer prayer when there are any idols in the heart.

What is an idol? It is anything that takes the place of God, anything that is the main object of our attention and love. God should be the only one to have the supreme place in our hearts. Everything and everyone else must be secondary.

Men often make idols of their wives. Of course, it is good to love your wife very much, but in the wrong place, she can be put before God. When your wife's pleasure comes before God's pleasure or you put her first and God second, your wife is an idol— and so God cannot hear your prayers.

Women make idols of their children. It is good to love your children, but when their interests come before God's interests, and they are put before Him, your children are your idols.

Reputations and businesses can be idols. If they are placed in priority before God, He cannot hear the prayers of that person.

If we want power in prayer, we must ask if God is absolutely first in our lives? Is He before my wife, our children, my reputation, business, even our own lives? If not, fruitful prayer is impossible.

God often points out idols in our lives by not answering prayers. This makes us ask why we are not being heard, and we discover the idol. Then we must put it away so that God can answer our prayers.

Ignoring The Poor

The fourth obstacle to prayer is in Prov. 21:13, *"Whoever closes his ear to the cry of the poor will himself call out and not be answered."*

One of the greatest blockages to prayer is stinginess— not being able to give freely to the poor and toward God's work. Whoever gives generously, receives generously from God. *"Give, and it will be given to you. Good measure, pressed down, shaken together, running over, will be put into your lap. For with the measure you use it will be measured back to you,"* (Luke 6:38). The generous person is mighty in prayer. The stingy person is weak in prayer.

One of the most wonderful statements about prayer, that we have already looked at, is 1 John 3:22, *"Whatever we ask we receive from him, because we keep his commandments and do what pleases him."* This verse is directly connected with generosity toward the needy. In context, it tells us that when we love we must not just say it, but put it in our actions. When we open our hearts to someone in need, then we have confidence toward God in prayer.

Many of us who are trying to find out why our prayers are so weak, don't need to look too far. It's because we are stingy. George Muller was a mighty man of prayer because he was a mighty giver. Whatever he received from God never remained in his hands very long. He immediately passed it on to others. He was constantly receiving because he was constantly giving.

When one thinks of the selfishness of the church, and how little is given towards foreign missions, it is no surprise that they have no power in prayer. If we get anything from God, we must give to others. One of the most wonderful promises in the Bible is about God supplying our needs. This was written to the Philippian church in connection with their generosity. *"And my God will supply every need of yours according to his riches in glory in Christ Jesus,"* (Philippians 4:19).

Unforgiveness

Now let us look at Mark 11:25 for the next obstacle of prayer. *"And whenever you stand praying, <u>forgive</u>, if you have anything against anyone, so that your Father also who is in heaven may forgive you your trespasses."*

An unforgiving spirit is one of the most common barriers to prayer. Prayer is answered when our sins are forgiven.

God cannot deal with us in forgiveness while we still have bad feelings for anyone who has done something against us. If we have a grudge against another person, then God's ears are closed to our prayers. How many of us cry out for husbands, wives, children, and friends to be born again, only to find our prayers are not answered? The answer is some grudge that we have against someone who has done something to us, or we think has done something bad. Some parents are keeping their children from being saved, simply because they hate somebody else.

Division In The Marriage

Similarly, we see an obstacle of prayer within the family dynamic. This can be found in Peter 3:7. *"Likewise, husbands, live with your wives in an understanding way, showing honor to the woman as the weaker vessel, since they are heirs with you of the grace of life, so that your prayers may not be hindered."* An unhealthy relationship between a husband and wife can block prayer.

A husband's prayers can be blocked because they don't respect, serve, and properly love their wives. The same can be said for wives toward their husbands. If there are unanswered prayers, married couples may find the solution in their relationship with one another.

A man can look and act very holy and is very active in the church and the ministry, but at home, the way he treats his wife can be unkind and harsh. Then he wonders why his prayers are not answered. The verse in 1 Peter solves this mystery. The same can happen with a woman who is devoted to the church and attends every service and meeting. At home, she neglects her husband, is irritated with him, focusing all her anger and harsh words on him. Then she wonders why there is no power in her prayer.

Other aspects of a marriage cannot be spoken of openly; these can also block prayer. A lot of sin between married couples can bring spiritual death and weak prayers. Any man or woman whose prayers are not answered should open their marriage before God; ask Him to put His finger on anything that he is not pleased with.

Doubt

The seventh obstacle to prayer is in James 1:5-7, *"If any of you lacks wisdom, let him ask God, who gives generously to all without reproach, and it will be given him. But let him ask <u>in faith, with no doubting</u>, for the one who doubts is like a wave of the sea that is driven and tossed by the wind. For that person must not suppose that he will receive anything from the Lord."*

Prayers are blocked by unbelief. God calls us to believe His Word completely. To question it is to make Him a liar. Many of us do this when we question His promises, and then wonder why our prayers aren't answered? How many prayers are hindered by our doubt? We ask God for something promised in the Bible, and then we only half expect to get it. *"For that person must not suppose that he will receive anything from the Lord."*

Study Questions

This is probably the most difficult chapter because it reflects so badly on us as Christians and as people who pray. It isn't easy to admit that we have at least one or even many of these obstacles in our lives. Going through these questions properly means being extremely open and honest with yourself and with God. It may even mean seeing things you don't want to see.

If you are ready, use Psalm 139:23-24 as a prayer to ask God to help you to see the obstacles in your own life: *"Search me, O God, and know my heart! Try me and know my thoughts! And see if there is any grievous way in me."*

1. As humans, we are all selfish by nature. How is it possible to pray unselfishly?
2. Why do you think many of us hold on to sin when God offers His grace, power, and blessing to us?
3. Make a list of the priorities in your life: Work, Church, Family, Sport, etc. Now put God into that list. Is he at the top—honestly? Are there other things you know that take first place?
4. Read Proverbs 19:17. How do you compare in the light of this verse when it comes to those in need? Now, read Luke 12:33-34. How do you compare to this drastic type of action?
5. What does it mean to forgive someone? Why do you think it is so hard for us?
6. Why is unforgiveness something God will not tolerate? (see Matt. 6:14-15).
7. Write down all these obstacles from this chapter. Put a rating out of 10 next to each one (1- no issue with this, 10- definitely a problem in my life). What will you do about this?

10

WHEN TO PRAY

For us to know the complete blessings in prayer, it's important not just to pray in the right way, but also at the right time. We can learn so much from Jesus' life.

In The Morning

In Mark 1:35, we read, *"And rising very early in the morning, while it was still dark, he departed and went out to a desolate place, and there he prayed."*

Jesus chose to pray early in the morning. Many prominent Christians have followed this example. In the morning, the mind is fresh and clear with no distractions. Concentrating on God, which is necessary for effective prayer, is easiest early in the morning. Additionally, if you pray before the day begins, the whole day is brought before the Lord— there is power to overcome temptations and to do what needs to be done. More can be achieved in prayer during the first hours of the day than at any other time.

Every Christian that wants to live completely for Jesus, should set apart the morning for meeting with God in prayer and studying the Bible. The first thing we should do every day is to be alone with God and get strength from Him to face the responsibilities and temptations that lie ahead. We should get the victory before the trials and temptations come.

The secret place of prayer is where we fight our battles and gain our victories.

All Night

In Luke 6:12, we learn about the right time to pray. *"In these days he went out to the mountain to pray, and all night he continued in prayer to God."*

Here we see Jesus praying in the night, spending the entire night in prayer. The Bible does not tell us whether He did this all the time or very often, but it is clear that there were periods when He prayed the whole night on purpose. If we want to follow our Master's example, then this is also something we should practice.

Sometimes, though, praying the entire night will bring nothing to our lives; because it is something we must do, and we do it only out of duty and legalism. But this is not an excuse to give up praying all through the night. We shouldn't say, "I am going to spend a whole night in prayer," thinking that we are doing it just to try and win God's favor— that is legalism. Rather, we should say, "Tonight I am going to meet with God to find His blessing and power for my life. And if He leads me, I will spend the whole night praying."

Often we will have finished praying before the night is over, and we can still go to bed in those last few hours and have a more refreshing sleep than if we had not prayed. Sometimes, God will keep us there in that place with Him until the morning comes. But the blessing and grace we find in such times are worth every hour!

Nights of prayer to God are followed by days of power with people.

In the evening, the world is asleep and quiet, and it is easy for us to be alone with God and have time with Him without being disturbed. If we set the whole night apart for prayer, there is no hurry. There is time for our hearts to grow quiet before God, there is time for our minds to be led by the Holy Spirit, and there is plenty of time to pray.

Praying through the night should be controlled completely by God. We should not have any rules about how long we will pray, or what we will pray about, but be ready to wait on God for however long it takes, and to be led in whatever direction He wants.

Before Important Events

Jesus prayed before every significant incident.

He prayed before He chose the twelve disciples; before He gave the sermon on the mount; before He began any trip to spread His message; before the Holy Spirit anointed Him and He started His public ministry; before He told the disciples about the death He would endure; before He died on the cross and fulfilled all he had come to do. (Luke 6:12,13; Luke 9:18,21,22; Luke 3:21,22; Mark 1:35-38; Luke 22:39-46.) He prepared for every important crisis with long periods of prayer.

We should do the same. Whenever any crisis or important event in our life is coming up, we should prepare by taking time to spend in specific prayer to God. We should take plenty of time for this prayer.

After Success

Jesus did not only pray before great events and victories in His life, but He also prayed after every one of these important achievements.

After feeding the five thousand with five loaves and two fishes, the crowd wanted to take Him and crown Him as king. But He sent them away and went up into the mountain alone to pray. Jesus spent hours there alone in prayer to God (Matt. 14:23; Jn. 6:15). So He went on from victory to victory.

Often we only pray before the important events of life and forget to pray after them. Remember, they are both just as important and necessary. If we pray after the great achievements in our lives, we may grow and experience much greater things that God has for us. But we are often too proud or exhausted by the things that we do for God, and so we don't grow or mature anymore than that.

Through prayer, many people have been given power and done amazing things in the name of the Lord. But after these incredible things have been done, instead of going to God on their own, humbling themselves, and giving Him all the glory and gratitude for what was achieved, they have patted themselves on the back. They became proud of what they have achieved. And so God chose someone else to continue in His plan.

When these wonderful times of God's work are not followed by humility and prayer, pride comes in and the mighty Christian is stripped of their supernatural power from the Lord.

In Very Busy Times

Jesus always had time to pray when His life became extremely busy. When the crowds were becoming too much, hassling and pressing Him for their needs, He would go away from them on His own into the wilderness and pray. For example, we read in Luke 5:15-16, *"But now even more the report about him went abroad, and great crowds gathered to hear him and to be healed of their infirmities. But he would withdraw to desolate places and pray."*

Some of us are so busy that we have no time for prayer. But when we look at Jesus, the busier His life was, the more He prayed. Sometimes He had no time to eat (Mark 3:20), sometimes He had no time to rest and sleep even though he needed it (Mark 6:31,33,46), but He always made time to pray. The more the work increased, the more He prayed.

Many strong Christians have learned this secret from Jesus—when work has become busier than usual, they have made an unusual amount of time available for prayer. Other Christians who were strong to start with, lost their power because they did not learn this secret. They allowed their busy lives to choke out prayer.

As a writer, I once had the privilege to ask a prominent Christian of my time some questions.

So I asked, "Will you tell us about your prayer life?"

The man was silent for a moment, and then, turning his eyes to me, replied, "Well, I must admit that I have been so busy with work at the moment that I have not spent as much time as I should in prayer."

It's no surprise that that great man of God lost his power, and the amazing work that he was doing, dropped off at an alarming rate.

We must never forget that the more work we have to do, the more time we must spend praying.

In Temptation

Jesus Christ prayed before all the great temptations of His life.

As He drew nearer and nearer to the cross and realized that he would soon face the greatest and final test of His life,

Jesus went out into the garden to pray. *"Then Jesus went with them to a place called Gethsemane, and he said to his disciples, 'Sit here, while I go over there and pray.'"* (Matt. 26:36) The victory of Calvary was won that night in the garden of Gethsemane. The incredible calm that He displayed during the aggression and antagonism at Pilate's palace and at Calvary, was the outcome of the struggle, agony, and victory of Gethsemane. While Jesus prayed the disciples slept, so He stood strong while they fell.

Many temptations catch us when we don't expect them and don't know they are coming. All we can do in those moments is cry to God for help. Still, many temptations in life can be seen before they happen or grab us; in those times the victory should be won before the temptation gets anywhere near us.

At All Times

In 1 Thessalonians 5:17, we read, *"pray without ceasing,"* and in Ephesians 6:18, *"praying at all times."*

Our whole life should be a life of prayer.

We should walk in constant fellowship with God. Our hearts should always be looking to God. We should be in His presence so often that even if we wake up in the middle of the night, it would be completely natural for us to speak to Him — asking Him whatever we need or giving Him thanks.

Study Questions

This seemingly practical and straightforward chapter can be just as challenging as the last one because it reveals how often and how seriously we take prayer. Don't be discouraged and feel condemned, especially if you hardly match up to any of these. The Lord's heart is that you grow in those areas to become more and more like Him.

Take this time to be truthful in your answers so that He can show you and guide you to where you need to be.

1. Are you an early morning or a late-night person? When is it easier for you to pray?
2. Do you think the Lord deliberately calls us to pray when it is naturally harder for us? Why?
3. Can you list any incidents when you prayed before an important event in your life? What happened?
4. Did you pray after the event?
5. Torrey makes an interesting distinction between temptations that catch us off guard, and others that we can see coming. Can you think of examples?
6. Read James 1:13-15 and discuss what you understand by these verses.
7. What is your idea of praying without stopping? Is it possible? Does the Holy Spirit play any part in it?

11

THE NEED FOR GLOBAL REVIVAL

To pray correctly and properly in our society today, a lot of our prayers should be for revival. There is no better moment and time as the one we are living in for us to cry out to God the same words as the Psalmist, *"Will you not revive us again, that your people may rejoice in you?"* (Psalms 85:6). This is certainly the right time for the Lord to work because people have ignored and thrown out His law (Psalms 119:126).

God's voice, as it is written in the Bible, has been disregarded and set aside by the world and the church. But this is not a time to be discouraged— those who believe in God and the Bible can never be discouraged. It is the time for Jehovah, Himself, to step in and work. The intelligent Christian, the watchman on the walls who is alert, might even proclaim these other words of the Psalmist, *"It is time for the Lord to act, for your law has been broken,"* (Ps. 119:126).

The great need of today is a global revival.

But what is a global revival?

It is a time when the gift of life is brought near, close, and quickly. Since only God can give life, a revival is when He visits His people. By the power of His Spirit, He pours out new life to them so that it flows on through to those sinners who are still spiritually dead in their sins.

There are many religious crusades and meetings cleverly put together using the appeal of a captivating, professional evangelist. These are not revivals— these are not needed. They are the devil's copy of a true revival. *New life from God*— that is a revival. It is a time when this new life from God is not restricted to one or two communities but is released among all Christians across the whole earth.

The reason why this is needed is that there is a lack of spiritual growth throughout the world. There is a universal death in the hearts of people. It isn't confined to only one country, although it may be seen in certain countries more than in others. It is found in mission fields abroad, as well as at home. We have had local revivals. The Spirit of God has breathed His life on individual ministers, in certain churches, in specific communities, but we desperately need a revival that is widespread.

It is good to first look at the results a revival can bring. These are very evident in ministers, the church, and the unsaved.

The Results In A Minister

- The pastor has a new love for the lost. Ministers generally don't have the love for unsaved people as much as they should— as Jesus or Paul had. But when God visits His people the hearts of preachers are suddenly burdened for non-Christians. They go out with hearts filled with the desire to see people saved. They forget about trying to preach great sermons and find fame, and simply want to see people respond to Jesus.
- When true revivals come, ministers get a new love and a new faith in God's Word. They forget any doubts and criticisms they may have had of the Bible, and begin preaching nothing but the Bible— especially Christ crucified. Revivals bring any pastors who are a bit too liberal or shaky in their beliefs to come in line with the Word of God. A genuine, wide-sweeping revival would do more to rectify all the nonsense being preached than all the investigations of blasphemy and false doctrine that have ever been held.
- Revivals bring to ministers new freedom and power in preaching. It is no longer a slog or nerve-racking effort to prepare and deliver a sermon. Preaching is a joy and a refreshment. There is power in it in times of revival.

The Results In Christians

- In times of revival Christians leave their worldly habits and separate themselves from that way of living. Christians who have indulged in the world, gambling, partying, watching whatever they like, and doing what they want to, give it all up. These things no longer mix with the life and light that is growing in them.
- In these times, Christians receive a new spirit of prayer. Prayer-meetings are no longer a duty but are necessary for their hungry, persistent hearts. Individual prayer is filled with new energy. Sincere prayers to God are heard day and night. People no longer ask, "Does God answer prayer?" They know He does. They enter into the throne of grace at all hours of the day.
- Revival brings Christians a change of heart for the lost. They don't just go to meetings so that they can enjoy themselves and get blessed. They go to see if there are any unsaved people that they can bring to Jesus. They talk to everyone they meet, at work and on the street with the cross, salvation, heaven, and hell as the main subjects of their conversations. Politics, the weather, fashion, and entertainment are not worth talking about.
- Christians have new joy in Jesus during revival. Life is joy. New life is a new joy. Revival days are glad days, days of heaven on earth.

- In these times Christians get a new love for the Bible. They want to study it all the time. Revivals are bad for movies and bars, but they are good for Christian bookshops.

The Results In The Lost

- First of all, revivals bring deep conviction of sin. Jesus said that the Spirit would convince the world of sin (John 16:7-8). We have seen that a revival is when the Holy Spirit comes in, so there has to be a new conviction of sin as well. If people are talking about a revival, but there is no conviction of sin, you will know that it can't be real. This is a very clear sign of a revival.
- Revivals bring conversion and new life. When God refreshes His people, He always brings sinners to be born again. The first result of Pentecost was new life and power to the one hundred and twenty disciples in the upper room. The second result was three thousand conversions in a single day. This is how it always works. I often read about revivals in different places where Christians were helped greatly, but there were no conversions. I doubt whether those are real. If Christians are truly refreshed, they will have hearts for the lost; and through prayer, testimony, and persuasion people will come to know Jesus.

Why A Revival Is Necessary

We have seen what a global revival is and what it does. But why do we need one now?

Just describing what it is and what it does should be enough to see that a revival is desperately needed. But let us look at some specific conditions that exist today to see the need for revival.

As we look at these, it can seem pessimistic. If facing the facts is pessimism, I am willing to be called a pessimist. If an optimist is someone who closes their eyes and says that black is white, wrong is right, sin is righteousness, and death is life, then I don't want to be called that kind of optimist. But actually, I am an optimist, because pointing out what's going on can lead to a better state of things.

In The Ministry

- Many who call themselves ministers are unbelievers. There is no other way to say it— it is also a fact. Tom Paine was a loud promoter of agnosticism and a fierce critic of the Bible. There is very little difference between his claims and what some of our well-educated Christian teachers are sharing. It may be sugar-coated and written in different words, but it is the same message.

A solid Christian professor of theology made some statements on a few things and asked his audience if they agreed.

When they replied that it was all good, he told them that he had been reading from Tom Paine's, 'Age of Reason,' a book that tears apart the very idea of Jesus as God. Of course, they were shocked.

Those who go off to study theology are being taught by unbelievers. Because they don't know any better when they go in, they graduate as unbelievers themselves, ready to be given a post in a church where they can further poison the congregation.

- Even when ministers are solid in their doctrine, they are often not men of prayer. How many modern pastors and preachers know what means to wrestle and spend the night in prayer? I do not think there is a lot.
- Many church leaders have no love for souls. How many preach hoping to save those who are dying without going to heaven? How many preach as Paul did, begging everyone to be reconciled to God?

It is clear that a revival is needed or some ministers will end up on that final day standing before God on the wrong side.

In The Church

- Look at the state of the church. Many do not believe in the whole Bible: Genesis is a myth, Jonah is an allegory, and the miracles of Jesus are questioned. Prayer is old-fashioned, and the work of the Holy Spirit is laughed at. Salvation is unnecessary, and hell is no longer real. Look at the cults and false teachings that have sprung up as a result: Christian Science, Unitarianism, Spiritualism, Universalism, Babism, Metaphysical Healing, etc.

- The church is filled with the world. Many Christians just want to get rich. They use unChristian methods to become wealthy, holding tightly to everything they have gained. There is a total lack of prayer. Some Christians don't spend more than five minutes a day in prayer. Neglecting the Bible is linked to neglecting prayer. Many Christians spend more time reading the latest news than they do in the Word. How many Christians spend at least one hour every day in Bible study?

- Along with a lack of prayer and the Bible, comes a lack of generosity. Churches are growing wealthier, but missionaries struggle to survive. It is shocking how little goes into funding missions. The Lord's Day has become less a day of holy service than a time of pleasure. The Sunday news is filled with scandal much juicier than reading the Bible; playing golf, running, and cycling; visiting and relaxing— all this has taken the place of church meetings and service to others. Christians take part in things that were once frowned upon. Parties, gambling, and X-rated movies are all okay now.

And how few Christians care or worry about the lost, carrying a burden for those not yet saved?

In The World

- See how few people are born again. Churches that were active in reaching out to those outside their walls have lost more members than they have gained. There are rare occasions where churches grow in number, but how many of those are real conversions?
- There is little conviction of sin. Very few people are overcome with guilt for disregarding Jesus' ways. Sin is seen as just a "mistake" or "a weakness;" but hardly as an offense against a holy God.
- Unbelief is rampant. Rejecting the Bible, faith in God and the idea of immortality are all signs that you are very intelligent. Maybe they believe it so much because it's the only thing making them look intelligent.
- With unbelief, we find its twin— evil behavior. They are always together and feed off each other.

Divorce is accepted and condoned; there is no issue for someone to get married many times one after the next. Thousands of respectable men are living with other men's wives, and thousands of respectable women are living with other women's husbands.

Entertainment with all its immorality is now respected as art. Theater, movies, and music all push the boundaries of sex and violence; those who perform in them are seen as great artists. Books are no different, as people will read something because it is the latest trend. Art is often just a cover-up for indecency.

Greed has gripped the rich and poor. The millionaire will do anything, even if it is underhanded, to become a billionaire.

The working man will go so far as to murder to ensure his living standards are kept. Wars are fought and people are killed to maintain levels of politics and finance.

You can see sex everywhere; television, billboards, adverts for cigarettes, shoes, bicycles, medicines, fashion. You see it on the streets at night, sometimes right outside the church door. It's not only in the worst parts of the city but in respectable areas— even in reputable homes. Broken-hearted men and women are a product of how badly the morals of society have slipped.

We need a revival— deep, widespread, global, in the power of the Holy Spirit. If it does not happen, the church, home, and country will fall. A revival, new life from God, is the only cure to stop the wave of immorality and unbelief. Arguing against it won't help. Only a sign from heaven, a new outpouring of the Spirit of God can succeed.

It was not a discussion but the breath of God that pushed people like Tom Paine, Voltaire, Volney, and other unbelievers to be forgotten. We need a new breath from God to bring down the accusers and critics of our day to the same place. I believe that breath from God is coming.

The greatest need today is for a general revival. It is very clear, so what shall we do? Pray. Take up the Psalmist's prayer, *"Will you not revive us again, that your people may rejoice in you?"*

Take up Ezekiel's prayer, *"Come from the four winds, O breath, and breathe on these slain, that they may live,"* (Ez. 37:9). Listen, I hear a noise! There is a shaking! I can almost feel the breeze on my cheek. I can almost see the great living army rising to their feet. Let us pray and pray and pray and pray until the Spirit comes, and God revives His people.

Study Questions

Torrey was passionate about revival. He wrote a whole book on the subject, with practical steps on how to prepare and manage one. This chapter is brief in comparison, but it is enough to get us thinking about whether we are passionate about it for our own lives, our own churches, and our communities.

Work through these questions.

1. What is your idea of revival?
2. Why is the Holy Spirit so necessary in a revival? What part does He play?
3. Torrey mentions a global/general revival rather than a local one. Aren't they the same thing, just on different scales?
4. There are some very serious issues in the church that Torrey brings up in terms of why revival is needed. Do you see any of these in churches you know? In your church?
5. "Arguing against it won't help." What will?
6. Where you are in your life, your state of prayer, your walk with God, are you ready for a revival right now?

Perhaps you want to understand more about revival or study some of the successful revivals and what happened, how they began, and the results. These are a few good books to read in that direction:

- Sermons on Revival by C.H. Spurgeon
- Revival God's Way by Leonard Ravenhill

12
PRAY BEFORE AND DURING REVIVALS

A book on How to Pray would not be complete without looking at prayer in revivals.

The first great revival in Christian history started in a ten-day-long prayer meeting. We read in Acts that the disciples *"with one accord were devoting themselves to prayer,"* (Acts 1:14) The result of that meeting is found in chapter two.

"And they were all filled with the Holy Spirit and began to speak in other tongues as the Spirit gave them utterance," (Acts 2:4) Further on we read that *"there were added that day about three thousand souls"* (Acts 2:41). This was a genuine revival with lasting effects. The converts *"devoted themselves to the apostles' teaching and the fellowship, to the breaking of bread and the prayers,"* *"and the Lord added to their number day by day those who were being saved"* (Acts 2:42,47).

Every true revival since then has started in prayer. The great 18th-century revival under Jonathan Edwards began with his famous call to prayer. Brainerd's marvelous work of grace among the Indians commenced with him spending days and nights before God in prayer waiting for power to do the work.

A remarkable and widespread display of God's reviving power was in 1830 at Rochester, New York, under Charles G. Finney. It spread through America, reaching as far as Great Britain. He said it was all due to the spirit of prayer at that time. There are many stories he tells about his experiences.

On his way to Rochester, a minister he knew jumped aboard the canal boat to talk with him and decided to continue with him. After arriving in the city and staying for over a month, this man suddenly could not help crying as we walked in the street. The Lord gave him a powerful spirit of prayer, and his heart was broken. As they prayed together, Finney was amazed at the man's faith in what the Lord was going to do in that place.

The man prayed, 'Lord, I don't know how You will do it, but I know You are going to do something mighty in this city.'

Instead of attending the meetings, other people prayed because the spirit of prayer was so powerful. Their urge to do so was so great.

Another preacher named Abel Clary, who had been born again at the same time as Finney. A quiet man, he hardly preached, because he became so burdened with the lost that he spent most of his time and strength praying for them.

Sometimes he was so overcome that he couldn't stand, only twisting and moaning in prayer.

Finney found out that he was also in Rochester when someone told him about a strange man staying at his house. The person said that Abel couldn't go to any of the meetings because he was too busy praying, day and night. Abel was often in so much pain that he could only lie on the floor groaning. The person did not know what to make of it.

Finney said he understood and that the man needn't worry, it would be alright, Abel would succeed in prayer. Mr. Clary stayed in Rochester as long as Charles Finney did. Clary didn't leave until he too had left. He never came out of the house— only remained there in prayer.

Another time while Finney was preaching in Auburn, he saw Mr. Clary's serious face in the congregation. He was with his brother, a professor of religion, but did not share Abel's God-given gift.

After the sermon, they invited Finney to their house where they sat down to dinner. Dr. Clary turned to his brother and asked him to bless the food. Abel bowed his head, but after only a sentence or two, broke down. He immediately got up and left the table. The doctor thought he was sick, so he went to check on him. He came back and said that Abel wanted to see Finney.

Finney went to the room and found Abel on his bed, groaning. The Spirit was making intercession for him, and in him, with groanings that could not be uttered.

'Pray with me,' he said.

Finney knelt and prayed for sinners to be born again. He continued until Abel calmed down, then went back to have dinner. He understood that this was the voice of God. He saw the spirit of prayer on Abel and felt it on himself as well. He knew then that they would see powerful results— five hundred people were born again.

Finney tells about other amazing revivals in answer to the prayers of God's people.

A devoted woman in the church became worried for sinners and prayed for them. As she did, she became more distressed, until she went to her minister. She asked him to organize an urgent meeting, but he would not as he did not see the need. She came again the next week asking for a meeting because she felt God wanted to pour out His Spirit on the people.

He refused again. And so she said, 'If you do not do it I will die, for there is definitely going to be a revival.'

He organized a meeting and said that if anyone wanted to know about the salvation for their souls, they should come. When he went there, he was amazed to find so many people.

In the fall of 1825 in Oneida county, another revival came about because of a very ill woman. She was deeply moved by the loss and troubled for her area. She didn't know what was making her sick, but she just kept on praying until it felt as though she would collapse. After a long time, she was suddenly filled with joy and shouted, 'God has come! God has come! The work has begun, and is going all over the region!' Sure enough, almost all her family were born again. The Lord moved powerfully across that part of the country.

The great revival of 1857 in the United States began in prayer and was carried by prayer. Most revivals start humbly with only a few ready hearts. Never look down on small beginnings— nearly every work of grace started this way. In Theodore Cuyler's church, one such move of God happened in a house at a hurriedly organized meeting. Another began in his mission chapel at a Bible study group organized by Mr. Moody.

The most powerful of all took place on a bitter January evening at a meeting of young Christians in his own house.

A remarkable revival occurred in Dr. Spencer's church because of the intense prayers of an old man who could not leave his room because of an illness. In Dr. Skinner's study, three men literally wrestled in prayer as they confessed their sin, and humbled themselves before God. Others came in and joined them, and the heavenly fire soon spread through the whole congregation in one of the most powerful revivals Philadelphia has ever seen.

In Ulster, Ireland, there was a great spiritual awakening in the seventeenth century. Holiness was rare after colonists with a love for wild adventure took over the lands from the rebel chiefs. Seven ministers came to settle there. One of them named Blair, who spent many days and nights in prayer on his own or with others, enjoyed a close relationship with God. Another, Mr. James Glendenning, was an extremely ordinary man, not the natural choice to lead a revival. But the move of God began with him; so all would know that it had little to do with man's work and everything to do with God's Spirit.

In Glendenning's preaching at Oldstone, many people were convicted of their sin. They cried out, "What shall we do to be saved?" As he preached, many could not stand and fell over as if they were dead. They were not weak-willed men, not scared to put up a fight. One of them had gone to the meeting looking to create chaos but ended up being born again.

This spread throughout the whole country; by 1626, monthly prayer meetings were being held in Antrim. Christians traveled thirty or forty miles to be part of these, staying there the whole time without getting tired, needing to sleep, or eating and drinking. Many claimed to feel even more refreshed and filled with the Spirit than when they arrived.

This revival changed northern Ireland.

Another great awakening in Ireland in 1859 began similarly. For two years, the need for a revival had been discussed and special prayer sessions organized. Four young men began to meet together in an old schoolhouse in Kells. Soon a mighty move of power began, spreading from town to town. The congregations became too large for the buildings, and meetings were held in the open air, often attended by thousands of people.

Often, hundreds of people were convicted of sin in a single meeting. Some criminal courts and jails had to close because there was no use for them. The Holy Spirit's power was seen in incredible ways, proving that the Holy Spirit is ready to work today the same as in the apostles' days. This is true when ministers and Christians believe in Him and begin to prepare in prayer.

Mr. Moody's incredible campaign in England, Scotland, and Ireland that spread to America began in prayer. Very little happened until men and women began to cry to God. The only reason Moody went to England was because of the prayers of a bed-ridden Christian. While prayer continued the revival grew, but over time people prayed less and the move of God rapidly faded.

One of the reasons revivals today are so superficial and cheap is because they depend on human intervention rather than on God's power— which is found through sincere, persistent, believing prayer. The great cry of today is work, work, work, new organizations, new methods— the great need today is prayer!

It was one of the devils' cleverest moves to get the church to put this mighty weapon of prayer down. He is happy to let the church increase in structure and techniques as long as it gives up praying.

He laughs as he looks at the church today and says, "You can have your Sunday-schools, Youth Groups, Men's and Women's Groups, Institutional Churches and Bible Schools, grand choirs and amazing worship bands, brilliant preachers, and even revival efforts, if you don't bring the power of Almighty God into them by sincere, persistent, believing mighty prayer."

Prayer can bring the same amazing results as it always has if the church would only embrace it.

Thankfully, it looks like some churches are waking up to this fact. God is laying a burden of prayer on individual ministers and churches that they have never known before. Less dependence is being put on techniques and more dependence on God. Ministers are crying to God day and night for power. Churches are meeting in the early morning hours and the late-night hours grieving to God for the latter rain. There is every indication of a mighty and widespread revival coming. There is every reason for a revival that comes now, to be more widespread than any revival of history. Technology and communication have enabled things to happen quickly and globally. A true fire of God started in America could spread quickly throughout the whole world.

The only thing needed to bring this fire is prayer.

The whole church does not need to be praying to begin with. Great revivals always begin in the hearts of a few men and women that God awakens by His Spirit to believe in Him as a living God that answers prayer. It begins with those few whose hearts He puts a burden that cannot be taken away except in crying out to God.

May God use this book to arouse many others to pray that the revival we desperately need may come— and come quickly.

LET US PRAY.

Study Questions

Often we read about such people as the ones in this chapter and we think they are just radicals, or that perhaps they have a special calling that does not involve us. As you work through these last questions, maybe your thinking of prayer has changed. Maybe your idea of you as someone who prays has changed. Maybe the expectations of God have become clearer, more urgent.

Allow the Holy Spirit to show you, to answer for you.

1. After having read the whole book, is Abel Clary's behavior in prayer strange to you?
2. Has your perception of prayer changed at all?
3. Are you able to pray in such a way as those mentioned in this chapter?
4. What would you need to deal with or change to move one step closer to becoming a person who prays—really prays?
5. Acts 1:14 and Col. 4:2 both use the word 'devote'. It is a strong verb that means giving all our time, energy, focus, and heart into something. How devoted are you to praying?
6. Have you grown in the area of prayer since beginning this book? If you have a desire to grow, it will be good to keep your notes and answers to all the questions and discussions from this book. In a year, look back over the issues you struggled with or had very little understanding in—this will be a good indication if you have matured in these areas.

ABOUT R. A. TORREY

As a student at Yale University, Torrey enjoyed the carefree campus life of dancing, betting on horse races, and going to the theater. Although he had been brought up in a Christian home, his ambitions were to succeed as a lawyer. One night, as he struggled with suicidal thoughts, the 18-year old boy cried out to God to save him. He even promised to become a preacher.

Reuben Archer Torrey is widely regarded as one of the brightest and most solid Christian scholars of his era. In his busy schedule of teaching, preaching, evangelizing, and writing books, his main aim was always telling others about Jesus.

"I love to preach the Gospel of Jesus Christ," he was often heard to say.

Having studied in America, he went on to further his academics in Germany from 1882-1883. While he was there, Torrey realized his error of having such a critical mind that questioned everything around him, including the Word of God. He began to see that holding on to fundamental doctrine was much more important to have a strong foundation as a Christian than the liberalism that was being encouraged at the time. Until his death, he defended the fundamentals— the basic teachings of the Gospel.

When he returned to the States, he was offered two positions: one at a wealthy Brooklyn church, the other a poor congregation in Minneapolis. Torrey ended up accepting the lower-paying appointment and with only a few members, reorganized it to become the Open Door Church. While in Minneapolis, he also took on the role of superintendent of the Congregational City Mission Society and adopted a phrase that would mark his attitude to all the work that he did: "Pray it through."

At the age of 33, Torrey was asked by D.L. Moody to head up the Chicago Evangelization Society. His success in the role was evident in the way he assisted in the curriculum and the practical Christian program, and he soon became well-known throughout the world. Torrey was the obvious choice to take over when Moody died in Kansas City during a crusade. He became pastor of the Chicago Avenue Church where prayer meetings and revivals seemed to be a normal way of life.

As an evangelist, he preached in Japan, China, Australia, New Zealand, India, England, France, and Germany, and other places, with thousands responding by being born again. In 1912, Dr. Torrey became the dean of the Bible Institute of Los Angeles. Even though the school grew under his leadership, he resigned to focus on evangelism in America, traveling extensively.

As a husband and a father, he was happily married to Clara, a woman who served, inspired, loved, and raised their five children with him.

As an author, he wrote over forty books, many that have become classics today. As a Christian, he is remembered as a man of prayer, setting apart hours to pray it through.

R.A. Torrey died in 1928, leaving behind a rich legacy of passion and dedication for Jesus.

REFERENCES

English Standard Version Bible. (2001a). Crossway Bibles.

Torrey, R. A . *How to Pray*. (Original work published 1900)

www.ingramcontent.com/pod-product-compliance
Lightning Source LLC
LaVergne TN
LVHW020425070526
838199LV00003B/278